Great Chicago Fires

Great Chicago Fires

Historic Blazes That Shaped a City

David Cowan

First Edition

LAKE CLAREMONT PRESS

www.lakeclaremont.com

Chicago

Great Chicago Fires: Historic Blazes That Shaped a City
David Cowan

Published August 2001 by:

4650 N. Rockwell St.
Chicago, IL 60625
773/583-7800; lcp@lakeclaremont.com
www.lakeclaremont.com

Publisher's Cataloging-in-Publication
(Provided by Quality Books, Inc.)

Cowan, David, 1963-
    Great Chicago fires : historic blazes that shaped a
city / David Cowan. — 1st ed.
    p. cm.
    Includes bibliographic references and index.
    LCCN: 2001089772
    ISBN: 1-893121-07-0

    1. Fires—Illinois—Chicago—History. 2. Chicago
(Ill.)—History. I. Title.

F548.3.C69 2001   977.3'11
                           QBI01-200492

**Printed in the United States of America by United Graphics,
an employee-owned company based in Mattoon, Illinois.**

05 04 03 02 01   10 9 8 7 6 5 4 3 2 1

To the families of firefighters everywhere.

Contents

Fire overtakes a furniture store in 1948 on Chicago's west side.
Despite the passage of time, the manner in which fires are fought has changed little.

Preface

Cross the hands over the breast here — so.
Straighten the legs a little more — so.

And call for the wagon to come and take her home.
Her mother will cry some and so will her sisters and
brothers.
But all of the others got down and they are safe and
this is the only one of the factory girls who
wasn't lucky in making the jump when the fire
broke.

It is the hand of God and the lack of fire escapes.

—CARL SANDBURG, "Anna Imroth," 1916

WHEN COMPARED to the ancient cities of the world, Chicago's history is short, almost embryonic. But in no way is it any less violent. Murder and mayhem had visited Chicago long before the advent of the Tommy gun. And so too had fire.

The word "fire" can trace its origin to the Greek words *pyr* and *pur*, which, according to most interpretations, mean "to purify." If this is the case, then surely the United States must rank among the world's most purified countries and Chicago its most purified city. As such, no history of Chicago can be complete without discussing the effects fire has had on the city, effects that have been both revolutionary and disastrous.

Firefighters often speak of fire as a living entity with a deliberate and sometimes cunning mind. Looking at the history of Chicago, we might believe it also to be an intelligent force, one whose flames have burned the city's wastes, mistakes, and embarrassments. Many volumes have been written about the Great Chicago Fire of 1871, a conflagration that stunned the city and the nation and forever welded Chicago and fire in the mind of the world. But the history of fire in Chicago doesn't begin or end in October 1871. In fact, when the "I Will" city emerged from the ashes of the Great Fire, it was following the example of an earlier Chicago, when the garrisons and entrepreneurs returned in 1816 to rebuild Fort Dearborn after it had been burned and its people massacred by the Potawatomi. Just as this, Chicago's first fire, illumined the faces of settlers determined but ill-prepared to face the uncertainties of the prairie, so too would future fires highlight the failings and frailties of an evolving modern city.

As the millennium turns, fire continues its role in Chicago's progress and change, lighting up a past culture: the factories, the warehouses, the multitude of ghetto flats of the "city that works" gone on to other things. Chicago is still burgeoning, but in different ways. Thus the story of Chicago and fire is a tale of the will and the courage to face shortcomings and consequences with a determination to reform, rebuild, and reinvent.

This book chronicles Chicago's other great fires, some of them headline makers, others not so famous, all of them valuable in the lessons they brought in the fields of fire safety and engineering, albeit at the expense of hundreds of innocent lives. A few common denominators found in most multi-fatality fires include overcrowding, inadequate exits, and lack of proper fixed fire protection. These factors were present in 1903, when 602 people, mostly women and children, died in the Iroquois Theater fire; and again in 1958, when a fire at Our Lady of the Angels school left 92 students and three nuns dead. These terrible tragedies brought to light deplorable public safety conditions and their worst potential, forcing the nation to assume its responsibility for improvement. Perhaps it can be said that in this sense the victims claimed by these and other fires did not die in vain, that their deaths helped make today's world much safer.

Acknowledgments

THIS BOOK is not a history of the Chicago Fire Department or of firefighting in Chicago. Rather it examines those Chicago fires that, because of their unique circumstances and terrible consequences, resulted in significant contributions to life safety improvements across the globe. As such, it has long been my hope that such a work may serve as a useful tool and a chilling reminder that no matter how advanced our society becomes, fire will always be with us, and that its power to maim, kill, and destroy should never be underestimated.

This undertaking first took root several years ago, following the publication of *To Sleep With the Angels*, an earlier book I co-authored with John Kuenster on the disastrous 1958 fire at Our Lady of the Angels School on Chicago's west side. Having been born in that parish, I had long been familiar with the story of the school fire; nevertheless, the toxic effect the project had on me was so overwhelming that afterward I swore I'd never write about fires or the death of children again. But something called me back and here I am, once more writing about deadly fires. Part of it stems from my endless fascination with Chicago—a city I love and hate with equal measure, the other the fact that, as a journalist and firefighter, I knew there existed an uncollected and important bit of history that needed to be told. Perhaps, too, were a few unsettled voices from the past begging for remembrance.

Every book has a writer, and behind every writer stand legions of people who make things possible. My first praise is owed to two friends and firefighting co-workers, Dennis Alund and Tom Gaertner, who, after plying me with a wealth of research material that ultimately made this project feasible, continued to encourage me to finish the job, particularly during those moments when I most wanted to put it away and instead write my version of the Great American Novel. Other firehouse friends forced to endure my mood swings helped me by simply being themselves and also by reminding me daily that the real heroes in life don't wear sports jerseys. Steve Murczek and Frank Sustr provided computer and electronic assistance while Rick Kogan, one of Chicago's last true newspaper reporters, gave insight and motivation. Thanks also goes out to Bud and Sandy Bertog, David Berger, Jack Kowalski, Joe Kissane, Steve Lasker, Scott Peterson, Larry Steffens, and Edward Prendergast, the chief fire protection engineer (retired) for the Chicago Fire Department, each of whom supplied photographs and information.

I am particularly indebted to Sharon Woodhouse of Lake Claremont Press for permitting the opportunity to publish and allowing me author's freedom, and my editor Bruce Clorfene, for enduring an exhausting read not to mention my inflated writer's ego. Together they made this a better book. Ivan Dee offered useful suggestions at the outset, and I also wish to recognize John Kuenster for being the best mentor any writer could ever hope to have. Friends and colleagues within the Society of Midland Authors continue to provide wonderful fraternity, especially Richard Lindberg, arguably the most knowledgeable crime historian in Chicago.

An abundance of thanks is also owed to the various librarians and research assistants who smiled and responded willingly each time I made a pest of myself. This is especially true of those at the Chicago Historical Society and the Chicago Public Library, particularly Andrea Telli of the CPL's Special Collection and Preservation Division, who provided timely organization to my repeated inquiries and archival requests. Many other people who deserve mention requested anonymity. These include helpful sources inside the Cook County Medical Examiner's and State's Attorney's offices, and the Chicago Police and Fire Departments. Other sources of abundant relevant information include the Office of the Illinois State Fire Marshal, the National Fire Protection Agency, the United States Fire Administration, and news reports published in the *Chicago American*, *Chicago Daily News*, *Chicago Sun-Times*, and *Chicago Tribune*. The archives of *Firehouse*, *Fire Engineering*, *Chicago Firefighter*, and the Associated Press proved equally helpful.

I would also like to recognize and applaud the efforts of Ken Little, Chicago's unrivaled fire historian, and his colleague, Reverend John McNalis, who, along with Chicago's large and dedicated community of fire history enthusiasts, have succeeded in their noble quest to establish a fire museum for the Windy City.

Lastly I would like to thank my family for putting up with the insanity that often accompanies a writer's life whenever a book is underway, particularly during the closing months. As always, Dolores and Adalbert Bielski were there to cheer me whenever I began to doubt. But it is my wife, Ursula, an accomplished writer and historian in her own right, who is most deserving of my greatest praise, appreciation, and admiration. Her insight, suggestions, and vast knowledge of her beloved Chicago gave me the confidence to bring this project to completion. And to Eva Grace, for always smiling and being Daddy's Little Girl.

Great Chicago Fires

Where there is sorrow, there is holy ground.

—OSCAR WILDE

*Come away O human child
To waters and the wild . . .*

*For the world's more full of weeping
Than you can understand.*

—WILLIAM BUTLER YEATS

Chicago in 1833.

From Dearborn to DeKoven

The story of fire in Chicago begins in August 1812. Two months earlier, the United States had declared war on Great Britain. At issue were maritime rights on the high seas and Britain's support of Native American tribes hostile to the settlers. After British troops operating in Canada captured the American military outpost on Mackinac Island, orders were received by the small garrison at Fort Dearborn to evacuate and flee east to the safety of Fort Wayne. On the morning of August 15, 1812, escorted by 500 local Potawatomi, the 148 soldiers and homesteaders of Fort Dearborn moved out led by a captain, three junior officers, and a surgeon, after destroying their stores of whiskey and gunpowder the day before.

Almost as soon as the journey began, the Potawatomi, whose allegiance had secretly been with the British, turned hostile, savagely attacking the evacuees at the Lake Michigan sand dunes near what is now 16th Street and Indiana Avenue. The small company of soldiers were quickly overrun and the Indians slaughtered and scalped as many as 86 adults and 12 children. Of those taken prisoner, some died in captivity while others were enslaved and later sold to the British and ransomed. The day after the massacre, the Potawatomi returned to Fort Dearborn and burned it to the ground.

After the War of 1812 ended in 1814, the area around Fort Dearborn remained largely deserted until 1816, when relations with the Potawatomi began to improve. Homesteaders reestablished the settlement at Chicago, and Fort Dearborn was rebuilt. One of the first settlers to return was John Kinzie, a Quebec native who had first arrived in 1804 but fled with

The rebuilt Fort Dearborn as seen from the north, 1816. The fort was abandoned in 1821.

Wolf Point, at the split of the Chicago River, 1833.

his family to Michigan after the massacre. The Potawatomi had spared Kinzie's homestead on the north bank of the Chicago River across from Fort Dearborn, a site formerly owned by French-speaking fur trader Jean Baptiste Point du Sable, a black man from the West Indies and Chicago's first permanent settler. Du Sable arrived around 1779 and over the years had built up a substantial establishment on the river, including a house, dairy, smokehouse, stable, and barn. In 1800, he sold his property and moved to Peoria. Kinzie died in 1828. As more settlers arrived from the east, a frontier town grew beyond the perimeter of Fort Dearborn. Commerce between the settlers and their Indian neighbors helped sustain both groups. Chief among the items traded were pelts, furs, guns, blankets, kettles, knives, hatchets, and whiskey. In 1818, Illinois was admitted to the Union as the nation's 21st state. Once the Erie Canal opened in 1826, Chicago had a water link with the east that eventually would contribute to much of its growth.

Though far removed from crowded New England, the young Illinois legislature took note of devastating fires that had wrought considerable damage to several eastern cities. In 1831, it passed a law authorizing any incorporated town to organize a volunteer fire company. Chicago was still a frontier settlement consisting of a dozen or so frame buildings. But following the Blackhawk War of 1832, in which the threat of any future Indian uprisings was quelled, the little Chicago village began to boom. Fed by a growing tide of westward migration, hotels and mercantile establishments began to spring from the prairie, and wooden sidewalks were soon running alongside muddy streets. So great was the demand for new construction that a carpenter in Chicago could earn three dollars a day, double that of an unskilled laborer. But prosperity brought danger: the wooden buildings were crudely built, and in their lofts were dry lumber and hay. Added to this was the wide use of candles for lighting

and hot coals and wood for heating. Given the circumstances, whatever other civic measures could be postponed, precaution against fire could not.

When Chicago officially became a town on August 10, 1833, its population consisted of roughly 150 inhabitants (some estimates place the population at 350) who lived and worked in 43 wooden houses and cabins built closely together along the south bank of the Chicago River. In November of that year, the town fathers enacted several fire ordinances, the first calling for all rooftop stovepipes to be insulated "by tin or iron six inches from the wood."[1] The penalty for non-compliance was five dollars. Benjamin Jones was named the city's first fire warden, and it was his job to enforce the law. The following year saw the burgeoning town divided into four wards, each having its own fire warden whose duty it was to make monthly inspections to ensure the stovepipe insulation was properly installed.

At the same time Chicago experienced its first officially-recorded fire. On October 7, 1834, a blaze broke out in a building at Lake and LaSalle Streets when a man dropped a shovel of live coals between it and another building. An account of the fire that appeared eight days later in the *Chicago Democrat* described the event: "Our citizens repaired to the scene of conflagration with a promptitude worthy of commendation and succeeded in arresting its progress, after destroying two other buildings adjoining. The wind being high at the time threatened the destruction of a number of surrounding houses, but by the exertions of our citizens were saved from the devastation."[2]

Among the buildings the fire destroyed were a cabinet shop, a grocery store, and a private dwelling. But despite the *Democrat*'s praise of Chicago's citizens who acted promptly to put the fire out, a stir was caused when the paper went on to criticize the lack of "suitable officers to take charge" of the fire.

The Sauganash Hotel, Chicago's first hostelry.

Two days later, Chicago's Board of Trustees met in the Tremont House to draft a new fire ordinance. This time the board named Benjamin Jones, the warden in whose district the fire had occurred, as chief warden, and the remaining three wardens his assistants. Each warden, like a sheriff forming a posse, was given the power to summon bystanders off the street to aid in fighting a fire. Another ordinance required business and dwelling owners to place at least one leather water bucket, with the owner's initials, over every stove or fireplace. This led to the immediate formation of the Chicago Fire Guards Bucket Company, the city's first bucket brigade. With so many buckets now in the town, in the event of a fire, every man who owned one could turn out and help under the supervision and instruction of the fire wardens. Another ordinance prohibited people from carrying firebrands or coals from one building to another, unless they were contained in an "earthen covered or fireproof vessel." A violator was fined five dollars, which could be imposed by any justice of the peace.

Although wooden buildings continued to multiply in Chicago, not until the fall of 1835 did the trustees order the first firefighting equipment for the city: two hand-pump fire engines, 1,000 feet of hose, two 16-foot ladders, two fire hooks with chains and ropes, four fire axes, and four handsaws. Even though the first engine wasn't received until late 1836, with the new equipment on order, the Chicago Fire Department was formally organized as an all-volunteer force on November 4, 1835. A chief engineer and two assistant engineers were appointed besides the four existing fire wardens. On December 12, 1835, the new department formed its first fire company. Commis-

Chicago's City Hall and Courthouse, with east and west additions, circa 1860.

sioned Engine Co. 1, it took the name Fire Kings and had its quarters on LaSalle Street where City Hall is now located. Pioneer Hook-and-Ladder Co. No. 1 was also organized during this same period.

Even with a volunteer fire department to protect it, the threat of fire in Chicago was still very real. Early nineteenth century fire equipment was crude; not only was it entirely hand-operated, the trucks had to be filled either by bucket brigade or with water sucked up from the river through hoses (fire hydrants were not in service in Chicago until 1851). The pumping of water was also very exhausting. Long poles were located at each side or at the end of an engine, and the normal pumping cadence was 60 up-and-down strokes a minute. Because even the sturdiest of men could keep this pace up for only a few minutes, a relief crew of fresh men would stand ready to take over. It was not uncommon for a man to break a finger or arm as he leaped forward to grab the moving poles without slowing the pace. In addition, in the days before fire horses, the men also had to pull the apparatus to the fire themselves.

When Chicago became an incorporated city on March 4, 1837, it had a population of 4,170. Because of the city's rapid growth of almost entirely wooden structures bunched up along crowded streets, a first priority of city trustees was to improve the fire department. The new fire chief, George W. Snow, who tried desperately to keep up with the steady expansion and erection of combustible buildings, formed additional volunteer fire companies. In most of Chicago's store-fronted structures, only the first floor was used for commercial purposes, while the upper stories housed dormitories for the scores of men that

moved to Chicago eager to make their fortune.

Not long after becoming a city, Chicago's second serious fire broke out on October 27, 1837, in a building on Lake Street near Dearborn Street. Eighteen buildings, including the Tremont House, where the board of trustees met to draft the city's first fire ordinances, were reduced to ashes. Though no one was killed, damage was extensive, estimated at $65,000.

Swarms of laborers continued to pour into Chicago, most of them to build the Illinois and Michigan Canal, an inland waterway linking the Great Lakes to New Orleans via the Illinois and Mississippi Rivers. When the canal opened in 1848, it turned the Chicago River into a crowded waterway of tugs and schooners. Commercial ships from as far as the Caribbean and eastern seaboard plied the river. The Chicago Board of Trade was organized to handle the sale of grain by farmers who now had greatly improved access to eastern markets. In 1847, Cyrus McCormick opened his reaper works on the banks of the Chicago River, and it quickly became the city's leading manufacturing plant. Railroad construction had also attracted many laborers. By the 1850s, Chicago was well on its way to becoming the rail center and crossroads of America. All

Buckingham Central Elevators at the Chicago River, 1855. Chicago supplied much of the nation with grain. Here ships and railcars await loading.

trains traveling between the coasts stopped in Chicago, and along with the waterways, freight trains transported much of city's industrial output to eastern markets.

As the city expanded, so did its potential for disaster. Most of Chicago's nearly 900 houses were made of wood, and fire insurance was haphazard at best. Historically, fire insurance evolved in the wake of the Great Fire of London in 1666, which destroyed 90 churches and 13,000 homes, and left four-fifths of the city in ruins. Up to then, fire victims were largely dependent on charity. In Chicago, a committee was formed to investigate potential fire problems of factories, lumberyards, and other combustible structures crowded in the central commercial district. The committee determined Chicago a poor fire risk. One eastern insurance executive made the following observation: "We should be very careful of what risks we take in Chicago . . . It is a new place and in all such there is generally a tendency of (placing) everything to the center."[3] In a sober note of prophecy, he wrote that in the event of another major fire, Chicago's central core contained enough combustible buildings to cause the destruction of the entire city.

In response, Chicago's fire insurance companies organized a board of underwriters to spread the risks and curb the practice of charging whatever the traffic could bear. Maximum fire insurance coverage was set at three-fourths the value of residences, and rates were set for each street. Insurance companies used fire marks of various designs to indicate to volunteer firemen that a building was insured, a practice modeled after that of the principal eastern cities: New York, Boston, Philadelphia, and Hartford, where it was common for insurance companies to reward volunteers who saved an insured building.

Even so, the destructiveness of Chicago's early fires was partly the fault of the volunteer firefighters themselves. Though members ranged from city leaders to workers, they were high spirited, rowdy, untrained, and beset with rivalries. Counted among them were loafers, thieves, bullies, and drunks. Many were drawn by the varying benefits of belonging to a volunteer fire company, which included exemption from jury duty, service in the militia (except in time of war), and payment of certain taxes. Though they were often heralded in song, poem, and lithograph, they were also looked down upon for being unattached rogues without any definite trade or occupation, but with a strong love for frolic and adventure. What's more, rivalry among volunteer fire companies was so fierce that it was not uncommon for one company to sabotage the equipment of another simply for the glory of proclaiming "first water" at a fire. Fire losses from looting had become so serious that a group of Chicago's insurance agents and businessmen recruited a special brigade of 100 men hand-picked to respond to fires and salvage valuables before the volunteer firefighters could steal them. Strict orders were also given to prevent firemen from tossing large valuables such as mirrors, vases, and other furniture, from the upper floors of fire-damaged buildings.

In 1855 Chicago's first fire alarm system was put into service, and the city was divided into six fire districts. Originally, volunteer firemen were summoned to fires by a bell rung from the tower of the Unitarian Church at Dearborn and Washington Streets. Then, around 1854, the loud bell hanging inside the First Baptist Church was used to alert firefighters. To signify a fire, the bell was rung eight times followed by the number of the district in which the fire was located. Early confusion was alleviated because the bell had a distinct hollow gong. This bell was moved to the tower atop the city's new courthouse, centrally located in a square at LaSalle and Randolph, where the main fire alarm office was based. A

24-hour watchman in the tower helped direct firefighters to the scene of a fire, hanging out flags by day and lanterns by night.

When the city's first annual fire report was published in May 1857, it showed the volunteer fire department boasted ten engines, three hook-and-ladders, 13 hose carts, six supply wagons, 6,500 feet of hose, five engineers, 670 enginemen, 100 hosemen, and 68 hook-and-laddermen. Impressive as they seemed, the numbers were deceiving. The test came on the morning of October 19, 1857, when Chicago experienced its most disastrous fire to date—both for the city and its volunteer fire department—at a five-story brick building at 109-11 South Water St., between Clark and Dearborn Streets.

The building housed a brothel, and according to most accounts, the fire began after someone knocked over a lamp. No lives were lost in this building, but the flames spread rapidly to several stores, warehouses, and rooming houses in the city's central business district. Before the fire was under control, 23 lives were lost, including ten volunteer firefighters, and property valued at $700,000 was destroyed. The first firefighter to die in the fire was 25-year-old John Dickey, foreman of Liberty Hose Co. 6. Dickey had been standing on the roof of a wholesale store, attempting to get water on one of the adjacent buildings, when its outer walls buckled from intense heat and collapsed. Several other merchants and firefighters were killed attempting to salvage goods from a building whose roof and upper floors had also collapsed and buried them.

According to the *Democrat*, the fire was started by "drunken clerks" who had been "carousing with a lot of abandoned women." As the fire spread, the paper reported, a half nude woman "leaped from a second story window into the arms of a gallant fireman."[4] Despite this praise, the damage and deaths exposed the inadequacy of an all-volunteer fire depart-

ment in a rapidly-growing city. A coroner's inquest revealed that, along with a lack of water pressure, Engines 6 and 10 had lost their hose before reaching the scene, and that neither company had repaired or replaced additional hoses damaged at a muster the week before, in which volunteers had competed for a coveted silver speaking trumpet. It was also shown that many of the volunteers were drifters from other cities drawn to firehouses as convenient places to sleep and drink whiskey. (Engine 6's headquarters was the saloon of its captain, Pat Casey, who never took the company to a fire without a case of "Casey's No. 6," a brand of whiskey that was said to make a man more daring.) Owing to the needless loss of goods to both flames and looters, when business leaders lobbied for a full-time, professionally-trained fire department, it spelled the

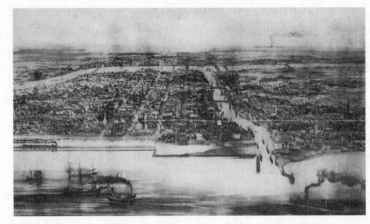

Chicago in 1855, with a population of 80,028.

beginning of the end for Chicago's volunteers.

In February 1858, Chicago mirrored several large eastern cities when it bought its first steam-powered fire engine. It was named the *Long John* after the flamboyant then Mayor John Wentworth, who had lobbied heavily for the new apparatus. A native of New Hampshire, Wentworth had been editor of the *Democrat* for 25 years, served 12 years as a congressman, and was twice Chicago's mayor. Just the year before, Wentworth had crusaded to clean up "The Sands," a notorious red light district whose tumble-down shanties played host to dog fights and sex shows. So fearful of the largely self-operating steamer were the volunteer firemen that they nearly rioted. A number of volunteer fire companies marched angrily through the streets, ending at the courthouse, where a near outbreak of violence was quelled only when Mayor Wentworth ordered a force of 200 police to the square. Most volunteers fled when the police arrived, leaving their apparatus behind. A police squad with a team of horses was directed to man the *Long John* in case of a fire.

The city responded swiftly. Within a month the demonstrating volunteer companies were disbanded, and in August 1858, a salaried fire department was formed under the leadership of Chief Fire Marshal Dennis J. Swenie, with each firefighter getting $25 a month. By 1862, the volunteers were gone forever.

Despite their abrupt demise, a grateful Chicago nevertheless recognized the sacrifices made by its volunteer firefighters with a white marble monument erected at Rosehill Cemetery in 1864. The memorial, the first of its kind in the country, pays tribute to the lives lost in the great South Water Street Fire of 1857 and to two other firefighters who died in 1859 and 1860.

As the 1860s drew to a close, Chicago had become one of the nation's most prosperous and promising cities. And by ushering in the horse-drawn era of fire steamers, its professional firefighters had shown themselves to be far more efficient and reliable than their volunteer predecessors. But the career brigade would soon be put to the test by the greatest calamity the city would ever know.

The monument in Rosehill Cemetery
dedicated to Chicago's volunteer firefighters.

This pre-fire photo
shows a typical block
in Chicago's central
business district.

Rise and Fall and Rise:
From Catastrophe to Renaissance

This is the one that's in all the history books, the subject of legend, whose anniversary is marked each year by National Fire Prevention Week. Though the purpose of this book is to tell the story of Chicago's other "great" fires, I must include The Biggie: The Great Chicago Fire of 1871.

Nineteenth-century America saw almost every major city come close to burning down, including New York, Philadelphia, Pittsburgh, Boston, and Portland, Maine. None stirred the nation like the Chicago Fire, which still measures the city's unique will and identity. Chicago may have been incorporated in 1837, but events in its timeline are qualified as having occurred either "before" or "after" the 1871 fire, making it the single most significant event in the city's history. The fire gave city planners and architects a clean slate on which to redesign a new city plan far more coherent than the original one that had sprouted up erratically and hastily in a time of largely unregulated boom. It also made possible the gem that Chicago is today with its open lakefront and systematic grid of streets, boulevards, and parks.

Much has been written of the Great Fire and there is no intent here to outdo what has already been exhaustively documented. But the conditions that caused such a destructive fire deserve repeating. And of course there remains the fire's universal appeal as the basis of one of America's most famous folk tales: that of Mrs. O'Leary's disgruntled cow kicking over the lantern. That the fire began in the O'Leary barn at Jefferson and DeKoven Streets is beyond dispute. But the rest of the story is now generally accepted as myth, fabricated by an unscrupulous newspaper reporter who capitalized on anti-Irish sentiment. Even though the Chicago City Council passed a resolution in 1998 formally absolving them of any responsibility, the O'Leary clan and their tragic matriarch Catherine were never quite able to escape the fire's stigma. Historians now believe it was probably an O'Leary neighbor who sparked the most famous fire in U.S. history.

By 1871, Chicago had grown into a major American city, the Queen of the West, thanks to the I&M Canal and the railroads. In just 40 years it had gone from quiet prairie outpost to a metropolis exceeding 334,000, the U.S.'s fourth largest. But if any city in America was destined to burn, Chicago was

Engine Co. 14, posed outside their firehouse on what is now Chicago Avenue, 1869.

The Chicago Water Tower and waterworks after the Great Fire.
These stone structures were among the few that survived
the destruction in the largely residential North Division.

it. Between 1858 and October 1871, the city experienced nearly 3,700 fires, eight of which were major loss blazes. This included a huge fire July 16, 1866, on State near Polk Street, which left up to 70 families homeless. The most destructive fire of the lot occurred September 4, 1870, when the seven-story Drake block at Wabash Avenue and Washington Street suffered a $3 million loss. This alarmingly high number of fires, 700 occurring in one year alone, prompted Lloyd's of London

to send a representative who issued a report that convinced the firm to cease insuring property in Chicago and to cancel its outstanding policies.

The drastic action was justified. Unlike London, which had evolved over centuries (and burned in 1666), Chicago was thrown up in a hurry. By 1871 it had expanded to 23,000 acres, nearly 36 square miles, with city limits extending west to what is now Pulaski Road, north to Fullerton Avenue, and south to 39th Street, containing 60,000 buildings, 90 percent of them wood. This concentration of closely-built wooden structures, including hundreds of miles of wooden streets, sidewalks, and picket fences, made Chicago a huge tinderbox. As the center of the country's woodworking industry its enormous fire potential was increased by an abundance of furniture mills, lumber yards, and paint and varnish shops, each combining to churn out thousands of wood-based products. Chicago also boasted the largest grain market in the world, storing its vast supply in 17 massive grain elevators built along the Chicago River, a waterway with 24 bridges. Several of the city's lumberyards dotted the riverbanks, whose dock areas were often clogged with up to 200 wooden sailing vessels. Despite this impressive growth, the city's fire department had failed to keep pace. The department employed only 216 men, including fire alarm operators, and maintained a small fleet of just 17 steamers and four hook-and-ladders, less than one engine per square mile.

The summer and fall of 1871 were hot and dry in the Midwest, causing a severe drought that left much of the region open to numerous grass and forest fires. Rainfall had only been one quarter the normal amount: only one inch had fallen since July, making the wooden city of Chicago ripe for disaster.

On Sunday, October 8, Chicago's understaffed fire department was exhausted. Since September 30, it had battled 20 major fires, four of them multiple-alarm blazes. The worst of these had occurred the night before. This so-called "Saturday Night Fire" burned more than four square blocks in the West Division, destroying property valued at $750,000. Though Chicago's largest fire to date, it would be eclipsed by the happenings of the following day.

The Saturday fire began between 10 and 11 P.M. at the large Lull and Holmes planing mill at 209 S. Canal St. in the boiler

Ruins of the Bigelow Hotel, one of Chicago's finest. The Bigelow had been completed and lavishly furnished just days before the fire. Its scheduled opening never came.

room. The mill stood in the center of the block next to several lumber sheds, coal yards, wooden outbuildings, and smaller houses and shanties. By the time the first fire steamers and hose carts pulled up, the mill was almost entirely engulfed in flames. A strong south wind quickly spread the fire to neighboring buildings, and in less than 20 minutes all of Canal Street between Jackson and Harrison was ablaze, as was Jefferson Street. The fire traveled east toward the South Branch of the Chicago River, devouring everything in its path. On the north, firefighters mounted a heroic fight that prevented it from extending beyond Adams Street. But the 17-hour battle had taken an enormous toll on both men and equipment. Along with lesser equipment, the fire had destroyed Pioneer Hook-and-Ladder Co. 1 and numerous lengths of hose, and severely depleted the department's supply of coal needed to power its pumping steamers.

The next day there were about 125 firefighters on duty, many of them badly in need of rest. Especially fatigued were several fire companies who had worked up to 22 hours straight. But if the men were hoping for a brief respite, they were in for a big letdown. Though they didn't know it yet, the previous night's fire was merely a prelude to the approaching apocalypse. At around 8:40 P.M., flames broke out about four blocks south of the Saturday night fire in the cattle barn behind 137 (now 558) W. DeKoven St. owned by Patrick and Catherine O'Leary. The O'Learys were a working-class family with five children; Patrick was a laborer, while his wife ran a neighborhood milk route. Together they owned five cows, a calf, a horse and a wagon, and property consisting of two frame houses and a barn in the back. The O'Learys lived in the smaller house and rented the larger to another family, the McLaughlins. The O'Leary barn backed up to a common alley and the fire spread rapidly beyond it, catching on to other adjacent barns and shacks. Six blocks away inside the Maxwell Street firehouse of Engine 6, *The Little Giant,* weary firefighters were trying to get some well-needed rest when Joseph Lauf, the watchman on duty, spotted the fire from his perch in the tower. "Turn out," Lauf yelled to the other six men in his company. Led by their foreman, Bill Musham, the crew quickly hitched their team of five horses to the company's Amoskeag steamer and hose cart. After starting the steamer boiler, they pushed out for the fire at DeKoven and Jefferson.

At 9:16 P.M., the spotter inside the courthouse tower north of the river saw the fire as well and struck Box 342, giving an inaccurate location of Halsted and Canalport, more than a mile southwest of the fire's position. Just as the signal was ringing across the fire department telegraph system, a passerby ran into the Jefferson Street firehouse of Engine 5, *The Chicago,* and Truck 2, *The Protector,* announcing that a fire was burning a few blocks south, opposite the location given by the fire alarm office. But it no longer mattered because by now the fire had grown so big that responding companies could see the glow in the sky and went straight for it. (Some minutes before, an O'Leary neighbor ran over to a nearby drugstore to turn in an alarm, but when the proprietor inserted his key and pulled the alarm box, the signal was never received at fire alarm headquarters. Three other alarm boxes in the neighborhood were not pulled until much later.)

Unfortunately, lost time and a fierce south wind had already sealed the fate of Chicago. Engine 6 arrived at 8:45 P.M. and got "first water" on the fire south of DeKoven Street that by now involved up to 30 buildings and shot flames 60 feet into the air. The fire, however, driven by hot blowing winds, was pushing north where Engine 5 set up and tried stopping it. But when its steamer ran out of coal, the flames jumped Taylor Street and spread from wooden building to wooden building. When

The ruins of St. Paul's Church.

Engine 5's pump ground to a halt from a lack of steam pressure, frustrated firemen tried stoking its boiler by ripping up boards from the sidewalks and fences, and even ran back several blocks to their engine house at Van Buren and Jefferson to get buckets of coal. But the fire didn't wait. It swarmed north across Taylor Street toward St. Paul's Church, feeding on the roofs and walls of dozens of buildings before turning into one huge sweeping arm of flame that was now poised to consume everything in its path.

The fire in the West Division did not extend west of

Jefferson Street or south of 12th Street. But the South Division, which included the central business, financial, and mercantile districts as well as Chicago's premier hotels, museums, and office buildings, was about to be reduced to ash. The same fate awaited the residential North Division containing the city's finest homes and mansions. Gale-forced winds turned the mounting blaze into a firestorm, and as the clock ticked away the rest of that Sunday night and Monday morning, the fire line expanded rapidly and the "Lightening City" of Chicago steadily disappeared. Throughout the burning districts, flying embers known as "fire devils" danced from rooftop to rooftop, turning night into day. Spires on magnificent churches ignited, then crumbled and crashed to the ground. Factories burst into flames. Sheds, barns, homes, and shanties were obliterated. Covering the entire city was a towering wave of orange that smelled of burnt wood and flesh. Said one fireman: "you couldn't see anything over you but fire . . . that night the wind and the fire were the same."[1]

Chicago had become another Rome, though no one fiddled as the city burned. No longer could the fire be stopped, only watched. By 1:30 Monday morning, it had reached the city's gas works, though thanks to a brave engineer, most of the gas had been diverted into sewers and a reservoir. By 2 A.M. the

Erie Street looking east. To the left, in the distance, stands the Water Tower.

courthouse, where President Lincoln's body had lain in state six years earlier, began to burn. More than 100 prisoners in its basement were freed and told to run for their lives. Five others convicted of murder were handcuffed and taken away by police. With its windows melting and masonry crumbling, the roof fell in, including the huge bell inside the tower, which on its way down destroyed the fire alarm office on the third floor.

In their panic to escape the city, people trampled one another. Even as they tried to outrun the flames, women stopped to give birth in the street, their labors induced by fear and excitement; some mothers and newborns burned to death on the spot. Many residents jumped in Lake Michigan or ran to the out-lying prairie. Others sought refuge in open graves of the city's ceme-tery, which at the time was being moved from Lincoln Park. When flames easily jumped the main branch of the Chicago River, it put to rest all claims that the river would act as a natural fire barrier. The army's attempts to blow up buildings in the fire's path also proved useless as fire stops. By 3:30 A.M., the gothic waterworks at Michigan and Chicago Avenues, five miles north of the O'Leary home, caught fire, knocking out all of the city's remaining pumping capability. When the water mains ran dry, hope was lost for saving the North Division.

to Lincoln Park and as far north as Fullerton Avenue. But it wasn't out-of-town fire equipment that finally brought the great fire to a halt. With nothing left to burn, upon reaching the prairie, it simply burned out. The last house destroyed was owned by Dr. John H. Foster along Lincoln Park. One more house north of the city limits did catch fire but was not considered within the burnt district. At 3 A.M. on October 10, a strong downpour extinguished whatever hotspots remained.

Chicago looked like a scorched wasteland. The fire had consumed a three-and-a-half square mile area—from Harrison Street north to Fullerton Avenue, and from the river east to Lake Michigan. Lost were some 15,700 buildings, including the entire central business section. About 300 people died in the fire, and 100,000 were left homeless. The exact number of

Though no photos exist of the actual fire, this image depicts the destruction wrought by its flames.

A coffeehouse in the city's burned district, one of 6,000 temporary structures built the week after the fire.

By 7 A.M. Monday, factories like McCormick's reaper works lay in a heap of ruins. All bridges over the river's south branch were destroyed while only two remained to take people into the North Division. Train depots and railroad cars were razed, but not before fire engines arrived by railway from other Illinois cities, as well as Milwaukee and Cincinnati. This equipment was sent into the North Division, where fire seared the homes of millionaires. In the end, more than 13,000 homes were consumed in the North Division, where the fire had advanced

A plaque inside the Chicago Fire Academy indicates the site of the O'Leary homestead.

deaths remains uncertain because many victims were burned beyond recognition. Others drowned in the river. Damage was estimated at $200 million, of which only $88 million was recovered. (After the fire, 60 of Chicago's estimated 250 insurance companies went bankrupt.) A few priceless items were also lost, including the original draft of President Lincoln's Emancipation Proclamation when the Chicago Historical Society burned. Also gone were valuable city, county, and business documents and records. Somehow, the wooden Ogden mansion on what is now the site the Newberry Library, survived. So did the frame house of Patrick and Catherine O'Leary, but not their barn.

How the fire began has never been determined. At the time, three theories were advanced. One was the famous legend of the cow kicking over the lantern while being milked. A second holds that drunk neighbors broke into the O'Leary barn to get fresh milk for an oyster stew, with one of them dropping a match or a kerosene lamp and igniting hay. A third suggested that neighborhood boys started it while sneaking a smoke in the barn.

The cow story has been debunked as a hoax concocted by a journalist. Most historians agree the O'Leary family was asleep when the fire broke out, as was their routine; they were working people and had to be up at 5:30 in the morning to milk the cows. Also without dispute is that at the time of the fire a loud party was underway in the adjacent McLaughlin house. Historian Richard Bales has suggested that Daniel "Peg Leg" Sullivan and another O'Leary neighbor, Dennis Regan, conspired to buy their way into the McLaughlin party with a tin of fresh milk from the O'Leary barn. According to Bales, when Regan went to find some whiskey, Sullivan hobbled into the barn, and while searching in the dark for a light, he accidentally dropped a lit match onto a haystack, sparking a fire that spread quickly.[2]

The official investigation did reveal that a woman's scream was heard in or near the barn just before the fire broke out, and that a broken lamp was found in the ruins the day after. But conflicting testimony from numerous witnesses rendered exact causes uncertain.

At the same time of the Chicago Fire, two major forest fires also erupted in the Great Lakes region, one in Peshtigo, Wisconsin, the other in Holland, Michigan, prompting some to speculate that a massive meteor shower may have started all three blazes. (The fire in Peshtigo north of Green Bay killed 1,200 and ranks as America's worst natural disaster.)

The homeless in Chicago camped out in parks or open areas with little food or shelter. Donations of money and food poured in from around the country, helping the city get back on its feet. To maintain order and reduce looting, Mayor Roswell Mason declared martial law and General Phillip Sheridan was placed in charge. Private police, including those employed by Alan Pinkerton, also patrolled the streets, protecting the wealthy in particular. Three days later the *Tribune*, whose building had been destroyed, put out an edition whose editorial read, "Chicago Shall Rise."

And indeed it did. Rather than wilt in the face of tragedy, the city's "I will" spirit blossomed. Just one week after the fire, 6,000 temporary structures had been erected, and within a year more than half of the old city was rebuilt.

In November 1871, *Tribune* publisher Joseph Medill was elected mayor on the "Fireproof" ticket. He served until 1873, and during his tenure oversaw a number of post-fire construc-

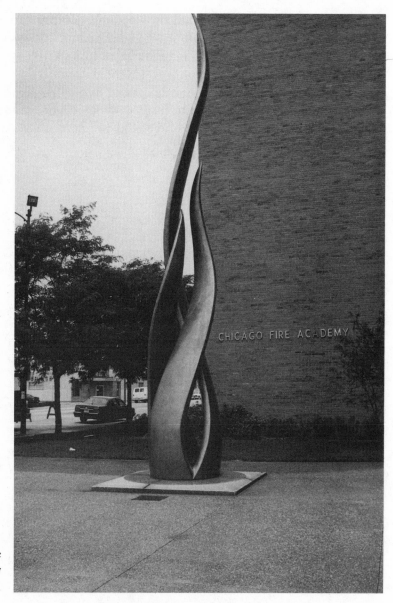

This sculpture of a column of fire outside the Chicago Fire Department Academy is said to mark the exact origin of the Great Fire.

tion reforms that included a ban on wooden buildings in the central area. Another major fire in 1874 burned a large swath of the central business area, including a notorious red light district, but paled in comparison with the 1871 blaze.

Catherine O'Leary died on the Fourth of July 1894, passing silently though unforgettably into history. Chicago's fire academy now occupies the site of her homestead and barn.

The motto "I Will" symbolizes Chicago's determination to survive following the Great Fire of 1871.

World's Columbian Exposition Fire

In the years following the Great Fire of 1871, Chicago had rebuilt itself into a great and determined metropolis. Its population had swelled from 334,000 at the time of the fire to more than 1 million by 1890. Railroads delivered settlers to the city from all over, and in time three out of every four Chicagoans were either first or second generation immigrants, almost all laborers who helped rebuild the economy. Chicago had certainly risen from the ashes, reclaiming its status as "Queen of the West." By the close of the 1880s, the city's new and impressive skyline stood high above the prairie. To show off these and other post-fire treasures, in 1893, the "Garden City" of Chicago made its formal debut by hosting the World's Columbian Exposition, a world's fair belatedly commemorating the 400th anniversary of Christopher Columbus's discovery of North America.

Competition to host the world's fair had been fierce. But Chicago's incredible post-fire growth and its commitment to commerce and culture earned it much favorable national and international attention, and it beat out chief rivals New York, Washington D.C., and St. Louis. Despite Chicago's reputation as a capital of vice and corruption, it was also known as a center of business, science, and culture. In 1890, the Chicago Orchestra, later named the Chicago Symphony Orchestra, began playing concerts in the newly-opened Auditorium Theater, while in 1892 the University of Chicago opened. During the same year elevated trains began running downtown, and one year later the world's first open-heart operation was performed at Chicago's Provident Hospital. When a war of words broke out during the intense lobbying to land the world's fair, Charles A. Dana, editor of the *New York Sun*, attacked the "nonsensical claims" being made by boosters of "that Windy City" of Chicago. Chicago won a nickname and the world's fair.

Since its earliest days, Chicago had adopted the motto *Urbs in Horto*, or "City in a Garden," and designed an extensive system of parks and lakes connected by grand boulevards. The fairgrounds were situated in just such a setting, on the city's unburned south side six miles south of the Loop and spread over a 700-acre tract of land abutting Lake Michigan in Jackson Park. Frederick Law Olmsted, one of America's foremost landscape architects, transformed the sandy, swampy land into a wonderful setting of lagoons and gardens that would host

Typical late-nineteenth century fire company, with wooden firehouse and dirt street. This is Engine 72 on Chicago's southeast side.

exhibits from 60 countries and more than 200 buildings. The fair cost the city $30 million and drew 27 million visitors during its six-month run. It turned a ten percent profit. Two prominent Chicago architects, John Wellborn Root and Daniel Burnham, were selected to design the fair's buildings. After Root died of pneumonia in 1891, Burnham decided to emulate classical Greek and Roman styles in his designs. Each building was built of wood and covered with "staff," a fibrous plaster substance that gave the look and feel of white marble. Thus the "White City" as it became known, appeared to be built of stone. The grand effect was further heightened at night when electric lights were played against the buildings' exteriors, illuminating the "marble."

A separate amusement area along the Midway Plaisance offered a variety of sideshows and games. In one tent, the belly dancer known as "Little Egypt" was said to take off all her clothes as she danced the Coochee Coochee. The midway also featured numerous rides, including George Washington Ferris's giant upright "Ferris Wheel," a contraption that provided riders with bird's eye views of the entire city and, to the south, the state of Indiana. The steel wheel rose 264 feet, equal to a 25-story building. It held 36 enclosed cars accommodating 60 passengers each. A single trip cost a whopping 50 cents and lasted about 20 minutes. Other popular attractions were Thomas Edison's moving-picture machine and the enormous nighttime shows of artificial electric lighting provided by George Westinghouse. When on May 1, 1893, President Grover Cleveland threw a switch to start the machinery, he not only opened the world's fair but also the age of electricity.

In addition to the stately show buildings, the White City housed restaurants, cafes, and sanitation and support facilities. One of the largest of the utility buildings was the fair's cold-storage warehouse. Dubbed the "greatest refrigerator on earth" because of its mammoth size, the six-story white terra cotta building at 64th Street and Stony Island Avenue had its own ice-skating rink and measured 130 feet wide by 255 feet long. And though not officially a part of the fair itself, the warehouse had been built specifically to store all perishable food items used by the fair's food vendors and to manufacture ice.

The cold storage warehouse appeared to be a sturdy, well-built structure, but it did have one fatal design flaw. Its iron chimney, fitted at its base to a series of boilers, was 200 feet high, and because it was considered unsightly and clashed with the beauty of the surrounding buildings, a large wooden tower, topped with an ornate cupola, was built to enclose the chimney and hide it from view. Herein lay the problem. The cupola had been built several feet above the chimney opening creating a dangerous fire hazard. The chimney was insulated by firebrick for only the first 70 feet; the remaining 130 feet were left completely open and unprotected inside the tower. Though the architect's plan had called for installation of a cast-iron thimble to extend the chimney above the cupola to protect it from the hot upward airflow, cost prevented it from being built.

This danger should have raised the concern of fire officials, especially after flames broke out inside the tower on June 17, although it was quickly put out by firefighters from the Columbian Exposition Fire Brigade, consisting of four steamers, two chemical engines, two hose wagons, two hook-and-ladders, and a chief. The Chicago Fire Department also maintained a battalion at the fairgrounds, including Engine 63 and Fireboat Engine 71. Named the *Fire Queen*, the boat was tied up in the park lagoon near the fair's Electricity Building. This combined firefighting force was headed by experienced officers of the Chicago Fire Department under the direction of Chief Edward Murphy of the 14th Battalion.

On July 10, the firefighters were called back to the cold storage building when another fire broke out inside the wooden tower. This time, however, the flames would not be so easily tamed. Led by their captain, James Fitzpatrick, more than 20 men rushed to the top, climbing interior stairs that took them to platforms above the hot metal smokestack. Using ropes, the men hauled up their equipment, including hose and a portable ladder. A crowd began to gather. Just then hot coals started falling onto a lower platform below the firefighters,

Smoke pours from the burning tower atop the cold storage building in Jackson Park, site of the 1893 World's Columbian Exposition. Twelve firefighters died in this blaze, most plunging 200 feet.

sparking a secondary fire that quickly burned upward. When it burst through the tower it cut off escape for the firefighters above.

The flames traveled quickly up the wooden tower, directly toward the firefighters trapped 200 feet above the street. To compound the situation, the water pressure in the hose line was severely inadequate, the pumps below unable to overcome the extreme height of the tower.

The stranded firefighters were left with just one option: they could tie off their hoseline and try sliding down it to safety. Though burned in the process, two managed to escape this way, to the cheers of the crowds below. When a third man followed their lead, he plunged to his death after the hose burned in half. A few others slid down a rope to the ground, but several more were trapped above when the rope burned as well. The remaining firefighters opted for jumping or falling off the ledge. The more than 40,000 spectators watched in shocked disbelief as the firefighters fell to their deaths. It took two hours for the 30 responding fire companies to put out the warehouse fire. Another three days would pass before rescuers recovered the last of the 12 dead firefighters, including Captain Fitzpatrick, whose body had broken through the roof and was buried in the debris. Fitzpatrick had survived the fall but died a short time afterward. Five other firefighters were severely injured, and one was crippled for life. Of the dead, four were Chicago Fire Department members and eight were with the exposition's fire brigade. Two cold storage employees and one electrician working in the building had also been killed. Property loss amounted to $258,000.

The tragedy, of course, marred the world's fair. Once again the Garden City was unable to protect itself from, or avoid being upstaged by, it's greatest foe: fire.

The next day, chiefs of both the city and the Columbian Exposition fire departments commended the "strong and brave men obedient to the call of duty and fearless of danger (who) . . . faced death before our eyes. While we deprecate the waste of noble lives, we recognize the steadfastness of true heroes."[1]

The iron chimney inside the wooden tower became a focal point of the subsequent investigation. The question of responsibility was never settled. But $100,000 was raised to help the families of the dead and injured firefighters.

The cold storage fire was not the last to strike the fairgrounds. In fact, it was fire and not the wrecking ball that eventually leveled many of the exposition buildings. Four months after the fair ended in October 1893, six buildings were destroyed or heavily damaged by fire. In July 1894, a third fire leveled nearly all of the remaining structures.

The 1893 Columbian Exposition was a principal moment in Chicago's history, its significance symbolized by one of four red stars on the Chicago city flag. But little remains of the fairground's existence in Jackson Park. The original Midway is part of the University of Chicago and is now a long grassy playground for university students and Hyde Park residents. The sole surviving fair building is the Palace of Fine Arts, a domed Greek neo-classical structure that, because it was designed to house valuable works of art, was built of sturdier material than its contemporaries. After the fair, it became the Field Columbian Museum and was used until 1920 to showcase artifacts of natural history. After an extensive renovation, it reopened in 1933 as the current Museum of Science and Industry. The only other tangible reminder of the fair is a memorial in Oak Woods Cemetery to the 12 firefighters who lost their lives in the cold storage fire.

EXTRA · The Chicago Daily Tribune. · EXTRA

VOLUME LXII.—NO. 313.   THURSDAY, DECEMBER 31, 1903—SIXTEEN PAGES.   ☆ PRICE TWO CENTS.

FIRE IN THE IROQUOIS THEATER KILLS 571 AND INJURES 350 PERSONS.

THE KNOWN DEAD.

Historic front page of the *Chicago Tribune* the day after the Iroquois Theater fire. It was devoted entirely to the names of the victims.

The Show Did Not Go On

"Absolutely fireproof."

That was how the Iroquois Theater, Chicago's newest and most beautiful show palace, was introduced to the public in late 1903. By all appearances the Iroquois was indeed a bright and modern example of fire-resistant construction, a building the *Chicago Tribune* called a "virtual temple of beauty."[1] But just five weeks after opening its doors, the Iroquois turned into a flaming death trap, killing 602 people, mostly women and children.

The weather in Chicago on December 30, 1903, was clear and sunny but very cold. The frigid temperatures, however, did not deter the holiday crowd from venturing to the Iroquois that fateful Wednesday afternoon to attend a sellout performance of the hit comedy *Mr. Bluebeard.* Many in the audience had come from out-of-town and were eager to see popular funnyman Eddie Foy perform his much-advertised elephant act. Officially, the Iroquois seated 1,600, making it the largest theater in the country. But with school out for the Christmas break, that afternoon's matinee performance played to an overflow crowd of nearly 2,000 people, 200 of whom held standing-room-only tickets. Patrons filled every seat and stood four-deep in aisles that stretched from the orchestra up through three balconies. Crowded also behind the stage were 400 members of the theater company—actors, dancers, and stagehands.

Even before it opened, the $1-million showpiece theater, designed by architect Benjamin H. Marshall and patterned after the Opera Comique in Paris, had been much acclaimed. Located downtown on the north side of Randolph Street between State and Dearborn Streets, the interior of the four-story theater was magnificently plush, with much mahogany and stained glass throughout. The dazzling lobby, with its ornate 60-foot-high ceiling, featured white marble walls fitted with large mirrors framed in gold leaf and stone. Two grand uncarpeted marble staircases that led to the upper balconies further enhanced the regal appearance of the entryway. Outside, the building's front facade resembled a Greek temple with a high stone archway supported by two massive columns. The archway was the counterpart of a monument in Paris commemorating the death of 150 victims in a fire at a charity bazaar there in 1857. The design would prove eerily prophetic.

To assure the public, Marshall had studied prior theater

The Iroquois Theater after the disastrous 1903 fire that killed 602 people and ranks, to this day, as America's worst single building fire.

fires, including the tragic Brooklyn Theater fire of 1876 in which 276 died, and made every effort to establish safety at the Iroquois. The new theater had 25 exits that, it was claimed, could empty the entire building in less than five minutes. In the event of a fire on stage or in the loft above it, an asbestos curtain could be quickly lowered to protect the audience. As an added measure, the Iroquois' management hired off-duty firefighters to be on hand during performances and provided them hand-operated fire extinguishers.

It all sounded impressive, but on the afternoon of December 30, 1903, the reality was troubling. Seats in the "fireproof" theater were wooden and stuffed with hemp, and much of the advertised precautionary fire equipment employed "just in case" a fire should break out had not been installed at all. The theater had no fire alarm, and there was no fire alarm box outside its front doors. In the rush to open the theater on time, several other key safety factors had been either overlooked or ignored completely. It was against this backdrop of greed and careless haste that tragedy struck.

At 3:20 P.M., at the beginning of Act II, the curtain went up and the house lights were darkened. Powerful spotlights created a soft midnight scene, bathing the stage in bluish-green hues as a bright harvest moon, projected against the scenery by another spotlight, started rising in the background. The audience applauded with enthusiastic delight when the orchestra struck up the overture to "In the Pale Moonlight" and pretty ballerinas costumed in blue and gold pirouetted across the left side of the stage. According to most accounts, it was precisely at this moment that a bright flash was seen near one of the floodlights over the right side of the stage. It was never known for sure whether the light came into contact with a piece of red velvet curtain hanging next to it, or if the light's wires overheated and arced. Regardless of its source, heat generated by the flash produced a finger of fire six inches long and two inches wide. At first the small flame traveled spiderlike across the edge of the drape, the fourth one back from the stage, then spread upwards, catching onto the oil-painted and highly flammable canvas, paper, and wood backdrops hanging by oiled manila ropes in the loft above.

Two stagehands working below saw the flame and reacted quickly. One found a long stick used to change scenery sets and tried beating it out. When bits of flaming curtain and scenery started falling to the wooden floor, an off-duty firefighter and another stage worker ran up and emptied two small Kilfyre chemical fire extinguishers on them. Other stagehands tried and failed to stomp the fire out. Burning debris continued to fall throughout the concealed backstage area, sparking numerous spot fires. In seconds, the small loft fire spread rapidly to the unprotected upper curtains and heavy combustible sets hanging directly above the stage. From this point conditions inside the "fireproof" theater deteriorated quickly as its auditorium began filling with smoke. The audience became aware that something was wrong when a flaming piece of drapery swung across the stage, causing the cast and several members of the orchestra to look up. But when smoke began filling the auditorium and large pieces of burning scenery dropped on the stage, the orchestra and the playgoers began abandoning their seats.

Eddy Foy was in his dressing room busily applying the final touches of makeup when the drama of the fire in the loft began to overshadow the production on stage. Dressed in his "Sister Anne" costume, he was due to appear in a few minutes opposite a comic elephant. When he heard the commotion he opened his dressing room door, ran to the stage, and saw the fire. Acting on instinct, he burst onto center stage and raised his hands, imploring the audience to remain seated and calm. "Ladies and gentlemen," Foy exclaimed, "there is no danger. This theater is fireproof. Don't get excited." He signaled conductor Herbert Gillea to direct the remaining six musicians to "play, play, play and keep playing." They struck up the waltz from Tchaikovsky's *Sleeping Beauty* ballet, which had a temporary, soothing effect on the crowd. After more flaming sets came crashing down onto the stage, Foy signaled a stagehand to lower the asbestos curtain to protect the audience. But the curtain snagged half-way down, possibly on a cable wire used to hoist a ballerina, or on an electric light reflector, leaving a 20-foot gap between the curtain's suspended bottom and the wooden stage floor.

The audience's escape down the aisles turned from orderly to panic-stricken. Foy's one last try to calm them went unheeded, and he fled to a rear stage exit. With hundreds of children in tow, the audience of mothers, fathers, grandparents, aunts, uncles, and schoolteachers scrambled for the exits. Almost immediately the aisles leading from the auditorium gallery and upper balconies became clogged and impassable. When the lights went out the crowd bunched up in blind terror and died at the exits and hallway doors that either opened inward or were locked shut to keep out freeloaders. With the auditorium filling with heat, smoke, and poisonous gases that made breathing impossible, children and mothers screamed for one another in the darkness and families became separated in the crushing stampede. Many children fell and

Interior view of the Iroquois showing the stage area where fire ignited draperies and spread quickly to combustible scenery props.

were stomped to death.

Backstage, theater employees and cast members opened a rear set of huge double doors which sucked a powerful wind tunnel inside, fanning the flames and sending huge sheets of fire underneath the open asbestos curtain and into galleries and balconies filled with people. A second gust of wind created a fireball that shot into the auditorium, incinerating patrons in their seats or in the aisles. All of the stage drops were now on fire, which spread to the entire auditorium, destroyed the 75,000 feet of oiled manila rope suspended above the loft, and burned the supposedly noncombustible asbestos curtain.

The scene outside the theater was unsuspecting and normal. Most accounts say the fire had been burning for at least 15 minutes before a faint wisp of smoke was noticed by passers-by. Because there was no fire alarm box located outside the theater's front doors, someone ran around the corner to turn in an alarm at the nearby firehouse of Engine Co. 13. Legend says it was off-duty firefighter Michael J. Corrigan, later to become one of Chicago's more notable fire commissioners; other reports say it was a stagehand. When the first firefighters pulled up moments later in their horse-driven steamers, hose carts, and aerial ladders, they thought it was a false alarm.

That changed quickly when they had difficulty getting into the auditorium because so many bodies were stacked up at the doors. "Pull a third alarm," yelled Fire Marshal Bill Musham, who had responded from his nearby city hall office. The men tore at the bodies with pike poles, pulling them down and peeling them off one another, clearing enough room to climb over. Once inside, they stretched their hoselines through the side doors or directly over the stacks of bodies. It took only ten minutes to douse the remaining flames because the intense heat had already burned up most of the combustibles. As the firefighters made their way further into the darkness of the charred interior, they were met by silence and the stench of burned bodies. "Is there any living person here?" one fire marshal shouted. "If there is any living person in here, groan or make a sound."

No one did.

The gallery and upper balconies had sustained the greatest loss of life. Here, the fleeing patrons had run up against locked doors that blocked access to the stairways. Firefighters found 200 bodies stacked ten high and a score deep. At the very top of the auditorium the audience had fought so fiercely to escape that they ripped the iron railings from the balconies, leaping upon the people below. Death, mainly from asphyxiation, came quickly to those who made it into the hallways and back aisles. But those caught in the auditorium were burned to death. Those who made it to the fire escape door behind the top balcony found the iron staircase missing. In its place was a railed platform that led not to safety but to a 100-foot drop to the narrow cobblestone alley below.

Across the alley behind the theater, painters were cleaning up from an earlier and unrelated fire in a building occupied by Northwestern University's dental school. When they saw what was happening in the theater, they reacted quickly, erecting a makeshift bridge of long painting ladders and wooden planks that they extended across the alley to the fire escape ledge. Reports vary as to how many it saved. One says 12 people crawled to safety, but that at least seven others fell to their deaths. Other accounts say scores jumped or were pushed off the ledge. Regardless of which is true, newspapers later dubbed the narrow area behind the theater "Death Alley" because of the 125 bodies found piled there—either from falling or being stacked there by firemen.

As the afternoon turned to early evening, bodies were removed from the theater at a rate of four a minute. The dead were covered with sheets and lined up on the sidewalk or taken into nearby stores where temporary morgues had been set up, including Marshall Field's around the corner on State Street. The victims came from 13 states and 86 cities. Chicago's 300 dead included 102 school children and 39 teachers. All but one of the 348 members of the Bluebeard Company escaped. The exception was Miss Nellie Reed, the principal of the flying ballet. When the fire erupted in the loft, she got caught on a tight wire and was badly burned. She died later in Cook County Hospital. Several families suffered more than one loss. William Hoyt, a prosperous wholesale grocer who had come to Chicago in the 1850s from his native Vermont, had lost everything in the Great Chicago Fire of 1871. But he started over, constructing a new building on the site of the old Fort Dearborn. This time the toll was more than material: his daughter Emilie and her three children, ages 15, 12, and 9, had all died. Hoyt's son-in-law, Frederick Morton Fox, never recovered from his grief, and he too died a few months later.

The next day, newspapers devoted full pages to lists of known dead and injured. A total of 572 had died, some of them never identified. Another 250 were injured of whom 30 would succumb in the following weeks. The heart-breaking death toll included 212 children. News wires carried reports of the holocaust around the country, and it quickly became a national tragedy. Because it was the end of December, Chicago Mayor Carter H. Harrison, Jr. issued an order banning any public New Year's Eve celebrations. Nightclubs were closed and the sounding of horns and the lighting of fireworks were forbidden. Every church and factory bell in the city was also ordered silenced. Two days later, on January 2, 1904, Chicago observed an official day of mourning.

An investigation of the fire and the findings of a coroner's jury brought to light a number of troubling facts. To begin,

because they had not been completed in time for the theater's scheduled opening, two pop-open smoke vents fitted in the roof behind the stage had been nailed shut to keep out snow and rain. These vents had been designed to allow smoke and poisonous gases generated by a blaze in the loft to be filtered out of the building. But because the vents were not working on the day of the fire, the products of combustion had nowhere to go except back into the theater. This fact alone contributed significantly to the high death toll by asphyxiation. Another finding showed the supposedly "fireproof" asbestos curtain that had been designed to protect the audience from flames was not fireproof at all. The curtain, which had been destroyed, consisted of cotton and other combustible materials.

And this was only the beginning.

Because there had been no pre-fire planning by the fire department or theater management, ushers and other personnel had no idea what to do in case of fire. Moreover, the theater had no fire alarm system, and sprinklers were considered too costly and too unsightly, not to mention unnecessary, thanks to all the other "built-in" fire protection. To keep freeloaders out and paying customers in, the Iroquois' management had quietly bolted nine pairs of iron panels over the rear doors and installed illegal, padlocked, accordion-like gates at the top of the interior second- and third-floor stairway landings. To prevent the audience from being distracted, management ordered all exit lights shut off during performances. One exit sign left on led to a women's restroom, another to a locked door on a private stairway. Those routes ended in fatal cul-de-sacs. Other exits had been covered with thick draperies. The doors of the outside exits that were supposed to enable the theater to empty in five minutes opened *inward*, not outward.

In the ensuing cover-up, officials from the city and the fire department denied any knowledge of fire code violations, instead placing blame on inspectors who allegedly overlooked the shortcomings in exchange for free theater passes. A grand jury indicted several individuals for criminal negligence, including theater co-owners Will Davis and Harry Powers, Fire Chief William Musham, Building Commissioner George Williams, Mayor Carter Henry Harrison II, a city inspector who had toured the building, and two off-duty firefighters who had been hired by the theater as fire guards. All were exonerated. Chief Musham did resign the following October after he was accused of failing to enforce fire laws at the theater. In 1871, he had been the first firefighter to get water on the O'Leary barn, and his resignation came on the 29th anniversary of the Great Chicago Fire. Families of the dead filed about 275 civil lawsuits, but not one dollar was ever collected because the Iroquois Theater Company filed bankruptcy.

With all the scenery, props, and costumes destroyed, the production of *Mr. Bluebeard* came to an abrupt end. But the

Engine Co. 13 in 1973. It was in this Dearborn Street firehouse, where, 70 years earlier, the alarm summoned firefighters to the burning Iroquois Theater around the corner.

theater building itself had been practically unscathed; structural damage came to $50,000. After repairs, the Iroquois reopened briefly in 1904 as Hyde and Behman's Music Hall, and then again in 1905, as the Colonial Theater. In 1924, the building was razed to make way for a new theater, The Oriental, which operated on the site until the mid-1980s, when it too fell into disrepair and closed. After an extensive restoration, in 1998 the Oriental reopened as the Ford Center for the Performing Arts, the anchor of a revitalized North Loop theater district.

Like many catastrophes, some good did emerge from the Iroquois ruins. Among the benchmark laws enacted in the fire's wake were those requiring outward-opening exit doors to remain unlocked from the inside and to be fitted with panic hardware. Other mandatory upgrades for theaters included exit lights, automatic sprinklers, standpipes, fire alarm systems, and flame-resistant scenery, props, and curtains.

The Iroquois Theater fire ranks as the nation's fourth

deadliest and the deadliest single-building fire. For Chicago, only one other calamity proved more lethal: in 1915 the Great Lakes steamer *Eastland* capsized in the Chicago River at Clark Street, claiming 835 lives. (Where the *Eastland* overturned is only three short blocks away from the site of the Iroquois building. Superstitious readers can note that each location is in the fire district of Engine Co. 13, which responded to both incidents.)

Like the Titanic that could not sink, the "fireproof" Iroquois stands as yet another monument to human failure to anticipate the consequences of haste and greed, not to mention our failure to respect the destructiveness of fire. Today the story of the Iroquois is largely forgotten, and no marker commemorates the site. Yet in theaters and public venues everywhere, laws requiring panic hardware on outward-opening doors, and lighted exit signs above doorways, can trace their origin to a cold December day in 1903 when the show did not go on.

Fire streams douse the ruins during the 1910 blaze inside the Chicago Stockyards that left 21 firefighters and three civilians dead, making it the darkest day in Chicago Fire Department History.

Disaster in the Stockyards

Poetically, it made Chicago the "Hog Butcher for the World." But in fact, it was an orderly center of slaughter and blood, arguably the most violent square mile of real estate in America. And during its 106-year existence, Chicago's storied Union Stockyards and Transit Company would see many extra-alarm fires, a number of them deadly, though none as terrible as the fire three days before Christmas in 1910.

Built on a patch of former swampland and named after the Union Army, to generations of Chicagoans it was known simply as the "yards," the place that for more than a century came to symbolize the city's working-class heart and soul. The stockyards opened on Christmas Day 1865 after Chicago's already prosperous meatpacking industry decided to consolidate its scattered operations into one central location. By 1900, it had become the city's geographic center and one of the largest industrial complexes in the world, employing one out of every five Chicago workers. With boundaries stretching from 39th Street south to 47th Street, and from Halsted Street west to Ashland Avenue, the 450-acre site held a haphazard jumble of wooden animal pens, covered runways, horse barns, and haylofts. Slaughterhouses, meatpacking plants, and office and show buildings occupied sturdier brick structures, some rising several stories. Crisscrossing the entire area were miles of railroad tracks enabling the quick transport of various meat products in refrigerator cars to all corners of the nation. Prior to World War I, when the stockyards were at their busiest, 100 meatpacking firms (Swift and Armour the largest) slaughtered nearly a half-million hogs, cattle, sheep, and horses. After being cut up, canned, and packaged, the output was loaded into freight cars and shipped out. Byproducts supplied material for other local industries, mainly leather goods, shoes, and soap, thus confirming the packers' motto: we use every part of the hog but its squeal.

During the stockyards' existence, tens of thousands of European immigrants and African-Americans labored long hours amid grim, savage conditions. Many workers lived nearby in quarters that ranged from brick and frame buildings to crowded, drafty shanties. The relentless stench of death from the daily slaughtering became a constant companion. Waste from meat production streamed through 30 miles of ditches and drains that emptied into a fork of the Chicago

Firefighters remove the body of a comrade from the wreckage.

river at 37th Street where it was carried to Lake Michigan. This small waterway became known as "Bubbly Creek" because it was so polluted it actually percolated from fermenting waste; in some places it had even solidified. In 1906, America learned of these deplorable conditions following publication of Upton Sinclair's *The Jungle*, which exposed exploitative working conditions as well as sickeningly unsanitary meat-handling practices. The sensational novel so outraged President Theodore Roosevelt that he pushed congress to pass the nation's first pure food and drug act. The stockyards then became notorious, a mandatory stop for tourists. Four years later, the Chicago stockyards would become the site of America's worst fire service disaster.

At around 4 A.M., December 22, 1910, Paul Leska, a night watchman employed by the Nelson-Morris meat packing company, was making his hourly rounds inside Packingtown, checking the company's two large warehouses on Loomis Street. The threat of fire was always present in the stockyards district, and during winter months, this threat was greatly increased because many of its buildings and sheds were crudely heated by pot-bellied stoves, fireplaces, and burn cans filled with wood and coal. Just the day before in Philadelphia, 13 firefighters and a police officer were killed when a fire swept a huge leather factory. So fierce was the fire that it crumbled mortar, causing the brick walls to collapse on the victims. Though Leska didn't realize it at this early hour, he was about to play a bit part in an even greater tragedy.

Leska discovered a fire in the Nelson-Morris plant No. 7, an enormous six-story cold-storage building on Loomis between 43rd and 44th Streets. After tracing the fire's origin to the basement hide room, Leska ran to the company's adjacent warehouse No. 6 and pulled an A.D.T. fire alarm. Someone else had seen the fire because at the same time a second signal was sent from a street fire alarm box one block away. The alarms rang at the two Chicago firehouses in the stockyards as well as the city fire alarm office. At 4:09 A.M., Firebox 2162 was struck, sending Engines 39, 49, 52, 53, and 59; Hook-and-Ladders 18 and 33; and Fire Patrol 4. Chief Martin Lacey of the 11th Battalion and 2nd Assistant Chief Fire Marshal William Burroughs also responded.

Engines 53 and 59, both horse-driven steamers with accompanying hose carts, pulled up minutes later and found the entire basement and first floor of the warehouse's northeast section on fire. What the firefighters didn't realize, however, was that flames were also spreading vertically inside the building through an open stairway leading from the basement and a service door Paul Leska had left open in his haste to turn in the alarm. Plumes of thick smoke billowed into the frigid morning air as the fire consumed the unprotected heavy timber interior and wooden floors saturated with layers of animal fat and grease. The absence of a sprinkler system allowed flames to spread beyond the basement and first floor, and because the water main servicing fire hydrants in the area had been shut down to prevent freezing, firefighters first had to turn on a feeder valve inside the local pump house to supply the hydrants. The delay permitted the fire to spread even deeper.

Chief Burroughs, a 25-year veteran of many stockyard fires, arrived with the first companies and, after quickly sizing up the situation, concluded the fire would be a difficult one to put out. The warehouse contained hundreds of head of cured hogs, meaning that saltpeter, a principal component of gunpowder, was probably present due to its widespread use in preserving and pickling meat. Many railroad and structural obstacles either blocked or severely limited access into the burning warehouse, including a huge seven-story lard house to the north and a windowless brick wall to the south. Another large

Another firefighter's body is carried away.

warehouse stood just west of the burning building. A line of boxcars was parked on tracks next to the building's loading dock, over which hung a heavy steel canopy that extended 15 feet over the tracks. Both prevented firefighters from using aerial ladders to open the iron-shuttered windows of the upper floors, permitting a dangerous buildup of pressure from the smoke and heat within.

As there was heavy smoke and fire in the building's east section, Burroughs decided to attack the flames through the two large freight doors on the loading dock. But because the boxcars blocked direct access, firefighters used portable ladders to climb over the boxcars. They then lowered themselves underneath the covered platform and set hoselines, first having to force open the freight doors that were locked from the inside. Meanwhile, the fire raged on behind the doors. At 4:42 A.M., Burroughs sounded a 4-11 alarm, calling out several more fire companies and Chief Fire Marshal James Horan.

"Big Jim" Horan was 51 years old and in his 29th year with the fire department. The last four were spent as fire chief, during which he improved and expanded the department. He arrived at the fire at 5:05 A.M., driven from his home on south Ashland Avenue by Lieutenant Joe Mackey and Engineer William Moore in a 1906 Buick—reportedly the only motorized vehicle in the fire department's fleet.

Horan met Burroughs on the covered loading dock, and after plotting their strategy, sent Chief Lacey of the 11th Battalion to the building's north side to supervise operations there. Burroughs and Horan remained on the dock where firefighters from Hook-and-Ladder 11 were attempting to chop down the wooden freight doors. So far hose streams had been unable to penetrate the fire

One of the few reminders of the Union Stockyards.
This former entry gate on Exchange Avenue is now a historical landmark.

raging behind them. As it got worse, Burroughs leaned over to Horan and said, "You'd better back down, Chief."[1]

Lieutenant Mackey, who had climbed atop the canopy, saw the warehouse walls begin to bulge from pressure building up by the fire. Mackey shouted a warning but he was too late. The enormous pressure created a violent explosion that shook the earth for several blocks. The entire six-story east wall moved out ten feet and dropped onto the loading dock, burying Horan, Burroughs, and a legion of firefighters.

With the adjoining seven-story lard house now on fire, First Assistant Chief Charles Seyferlich called the first special alarm at 5:12 A.M. summoning 50 engines, seven hook-and-ladders, and numerous special apparatus. Two hundred off-duty firemen from the next shift reported, many arriving by streetcar. For 16 hours the buildings burned, threatening at one point to ignite the adjacent Armour Co. plant. Gradually the flames were brought under control, and firefighters were able to concentrate on finding their lost brothers amid the avalanche of broken bricks and heavy timbers.

As the collapsed building still smoldered, a railroad wrecking train and a steam shovel were wheeled in to dig through its charred remains. Working amid snow and freezing temperatures, rescuers sifted through tons of rubble with gloved hands. More than 50 firefighters dropped

from exhaustion. But one by one, the badly burned and mutilated bodies were recovered. Relatives were informed as each was identified. Chief Horan's remains weren't found until 9:35 that evening. His white helmet had been spotted first,

The disaster site today.

then his body was located 15 feet from where he had been standing, seated face forward, his arms folded across his chest. A heavy beam had fallen over the chief's right leg, nearly severing it. His back and skull had been crushed, but his face had hardly been cut. Horan was taken to the funeral parlor owned by his brother, Daniel Horan, at 307 E. 61st St., about two miles away. It was reported that Mayor Fred Busse, upon viewing the body of his old friend, had wept for some time.

Meanwhile, fire companies worked for more than 26 hours straight before the fire was declared struck out and the final body located. One firefighter carried away from grief and fatigue was Pipeman Edward Doyle, who had spent hours digging through the ruins and praying for a miracle. He collapsed after the last body was recovered—that of his missing father, Captain Dennis Doyle, commander of Engine 39. Captain Doyle's other son, Nicholas Doyle, a member of Hook-and-Ladder 11, had also been killed along with his entire company.

Compared to the human toll, the $400,000 in property loss was minimal. Twenty-one city firefighters had been killed that day, including Chief Horan, Second Assistant Chief Burroughs, three captains, four lieutenants, 11 pipemen and laddermen, and one driver. Three civilians—a railroad worker and two Nelson-Morris employees—had also lost their lives. Fifteen other firemen were injured, many critically. (Chief Lacey narrowly escaped death, suffering only a broken leg. But fate would catch up with him six years later when, in November 1916, he was killed in a vehicle collision while responding to another fire in the stockyards.)

One firefighter who had been reported killed shocked his grieving wife when he returned home unharmed many hours later. Other wives were not so lucky. A number of personal circumstances heightened the tragedy for several families. Lieutenant Herman Brandenberg of Hook-and-Ladder 11 was working his day off so he could be home Christmas Day. Lieutenant James Fitzgerald, 33, was to be married Christmas Eve, while another dead firefighter was to have celebrated his third wedding anniversary the same day. Firefighter Edward Schonsett's death came on his 27th birthday. Firefighter William Weber had just moved into a new house with his large family and was to celebrate a special holiday dinner to mark the event.

The catastrophe stunned not only the local populace but shook the entire nation as well, especially since it came on the heels of Philadelphia's tragedy. Instead of celebrating Christmas and the coming New Year, families had to bury their dead members, which eight of them did on Christmas Day alone. Chief Horan's funeral mass was held the following day at Holy Name Cathedral and co-celebrated by Archbishop Quigley. During the eulogy, Rev. Peter J. O'Callaghan called Horan a "big, full-blooded man who enjoyed life and wasn't afraid to die."[2] Among the chief's pallbearers was Captain Michael J. Corrigan of Engine Co. 104, later to become one of Chicago's legendary fire commissioners.

An inquest into the stockyards fire speculated that an electrical short in a basement switch box of the Nelson-Morris building caused an arc that ignited combustible materials stored in the hide room after past fire inspections found deficiencies in the building's electrical system, such as overheated high voltage wires. Low water pressure was also cited as a factor that hampered firefighter's efforts, enabling the fire to reach great proportions. No ammonia was stored in the building despite earlier suspicions stemming from its widespread use in meat pickling.

The 1910 stockyards fire ranks not only as the darkest day in the history of the Chicago Fire Department, but also stands among the largest single losses of American firefighters. After the fire, a death mask was made of Chief Horan, but a planned statue of his likeness never materialized. A plaque honoring the 21 fallen men hangs inside fire department headquarters in

Chicago's City Hall.

Engine 95 in Garfield Park, a typical fire engine serving Chicago in the 1920s.

The Hand of Death

In 1924, Good Friday fell on April 18. On that afternoon, members of the Chicago Fire Department's Engine Co. 107 and Truck Co. 12 settled into their daily routine. Even though it was a holy day, cleaning the large firehouse was still a necessary duty. After drawing the task of cleaning the first-floor windows, Francis X. Leavy, a member of Engine 107, set about his duties without any specific zeal.

At that particular moment in history, the world beyond the stable pattern of firehouse life was pursuing an unusually lively pace. Europe was still rebuilding from the Great War. In Paris, a lost generation of writers and artists was trying to make sense of it all. In America, the Roaring Twenties moved wildly to the playing of Benny Goodman and Louis Armstrong. It was the Jazz Age, an era of flappers and It Girls, of illegal liquor and underground speakeasies, of individual fortunes created by a skyrocketing stock market. Chicago was in the thick of the action, a Babylon of prostitution, gambling, and bootlegging thanks largely to its mayor and chief buffoon, William Hale "Big Bill" Thompson, who along with most city cops and county judges, was compensated handsomely by the underworld. In 1924, Chicago's Grant Park Stadium was renamed Soldier Field in honor of America's World War I veterans, and a reform mayor, William Devers, was elected after promising to clean things up. But four years later the crooked Thompson would be back in office, once again padding his pockets with the spoils of public corruption.

Frank Leavy and his Chicago Fire Department colleagues didn't share in the glamour of the era. As gangster Al Capone lived a potentate's existence in downtown Chicago hotel suites, city firemen struggled to raise families on about $2,500 a year. Most had to work second jobs. Frank Leavy spent his days off driving a taxi.

Like most of his co-workers, Leavy was Irish. He joined the fire department 13 years earlier after an eight-year stint in the navy, which he had joined at age 14. A family man, he and his wife Mary were parents of a young son and daughter, Frank, Jr. and June. When Leavy said goodbye that Good Friday morning, no one guessed it would be for the last time. All day, the normally upbeat Leavy seemed uncharacteristically sullen, even melancholy.

As the firemen went about their cleaning, they listened to the Joker, the telegraph system at the front of the firehouse that devoted most of that afternoon to a four-alarm fire in the Union Stockyards. The fire was too far away; Engine 107 and Truck 12 were not due to respond. Yet, that such a large fire was burning only a few miles to the south made the men edgy. Leavy tried putting it out of his mind, concentrating on the window he was washing. He placed his left hand against the glass and wiped it clean with a soapy sponge in his right hand. It was precisely at this moment that he looked down and uttered a grim prophecy:

"This is my last day on the fire department."[1]

Though Leavy had spoken to no one in particular, his words, coupled with his sudden change in personality, puzzled his fellow firefighters, including Edward McKevitt, who had been standing next to him. Before McKevitt could respond, bells started ringing. Box 372 was coming in for a fire a mile-and-a-half east. Engine 107 and Truck 12 were due to cover the response because other fire companies stationed closer to the new fire were fighting the stockyards fire. "Fourteenth and Blue Island," yelled the officer at the desk. "Let's Go."[2] Leavy donned his boots, coat, and helmet and jumped on the back of the 1921 Ahrens-Fox pumper assigned to Engine 107.

The fire was bad. Burning was Curran Hall, a landmark 50-year-old brick building at 1363 S. Blue Island, southwest of the Loop. During its heyday, the four-story dance hall had been a popular party spot. But thanks to time and Prohibition, instead of dancing and fun, the hall now was home to several small businesses, including a leather goods store.

Engine 107's crew stretched a hoseline up the fire escape and into the burning second floor. They crawled on hands and knees through the heat and blinding smoke, inching their way to the seat of the fire. In those days firefighters had no breathing apparatus, so they had to follow the hose and crawl

back and forth to the door to grab a breath of fresh air. After playing water against the flames for about a half hour, it began to darken, but the firefighters could sense something was wrong. Their instincts were confirmed when fire commanders outside began frantically screaming for their men to get out of the building.

But the warning came too late because no sooner did the men from Engine 107 and Truck 12 begin scrambling for the fire escape when the building's outer walls buckled, bringing down the entire structure, burying the firefighters inside. The collapse knocked out electrical power to the area, leaving those searching for trapped men to use flashlights. For several hours they dug by hand amid the possibility of a secondary collapse. When cranes were finally brought in eight bodies were dug out. Frank Leavy's dire prophecy had been fulfilled: he had been among those killed. Though Leavy's chest had been severely crushed, his was the only body recovered with an intact face, its features clearly distinguishable.

Of the eight dead firefighters, six were from the firehouse at 13th and Oakley. One civilian had also been killed. A ninth firefighter, also from the Oakley station, died eight days later. Twenty others had been injured. A tenth firefighter suffered a fatal heart attack while serving as a pallbearer for one of the victims from Truck 12.

When the building collapsed, Edward McKevitt was working outside. The next day, the shaken McKevitt related to a group of firefighters Leavy's spooky premonition of death. As he told the story, McKevitt glanced up at the window Leavy had been wiping. Etched in the glass, in the exact spot where Leavy had rested his soapy left hand was the image of a man's handprint. Because it hadn't been there before, McKevitt suggested the handprint was Leavy's, and he and the others tried scrubbing it away. When the image refused to come off, a combination of fear and mystery infiltrated the firehouse.

Arson surfaced during the investigation of the Curran Hall fire. Flammable liquids had been used to start the fire, which originated inside the leather goods store on the second floor. Detectives learned that the store's two owners had been in financial trouble, and that on the night of the fire, the pair had instructed their employees not to lock the rear doors. Witnesses later related seeing one of the men leave the building through the unlocked door shortly before the fire was reported. After a coroner's jury returned a verdict of murder by arson, the two owners were indicted. At trial the defendants were acquitted because, despite an abundance of circumstantial evidence, nothing could be produced to prove that they had actually started the fire themselves. For the dead firefighters and their families, this meant justice had been denied.

Meanwhile, the legend of the ghostly handprint lived on. Over the years, firefighters assigned to Engine 107 and Truck 12 came and went. But in the course of their daily house duties, many had tried to scrub the mysterious handprint from the window. Not one effort, including the use of ammonia or scraping the glass

A fire department water tower working a 5-alarm fire at Clinton and Madison Streets in January 1936. The temperature on this day was seven degrees below zero.

with a razor blade, had succeeded. Finally, the Pittsburgh Glass Company, which had manufactured the window, was called in. Still, the apparently supernatural print resisted even their toughest chemical cleaning compounds, causing the handprint to become all the more famous. Dozens of people visited the firehouse to view the strange phenomenon and listen to the story of Frank Leavy. Was the handprint an apparition? No one knew for sure. But when a city official obtained a copy of Leavy's thumbprint, it was compared with the print on the window. The two thumbprints matched perfectly. There could be no doubt: the handprint on the glass definitely belonged to Frank Leavy.

The handprint remained undisturbed for 20 years until one day in 1944, when the unexplained revisited the firehouse at 13th and Oakley. A newsboy accidentally threw the afternoon paper through the window, shattering the glass containing the handprint along with any hope of solving its mystery or preserving its physical evidence. What made the accident eerie was the date of its occurrence: April 18, 1944, exactly 20 years to the day of Leavy's death.

Leavy's widow, Mary, and her daughter, June, never went to the firehouse to view the handprint. The

Fire clears a part of Chicago's industrial landscape. This Halloween 1978 fire destroyed a factory on the west side.

younger Frank Leavy did, though he never conceded that the print was his father's. Yet, he did follow in his father's footsteps by joining the Chicago Fire Department on April 18, 1945, the 21st anniversary of his father's death. He was not assigned to Engine 107.

Aside from the belief that the handprint was supernatural, some have theorized that Frank Leavy's fear of an impending crisis may have caused his pancreas to produce a chemical that left behind a permanent stain through his perspiration. No one will ever know for sure. The firehouse at 13th and Oakley was razed in 1971, replaced by a newer one a few blocks away.

The Chicago Stockyards around 1930. Most of the wooden cattle pens and runways in the foreground were destroyed in the 1934 fire.

Hog Butcher to the World

After the stock market crash of October 1929, the glittery 1920s yielded to the Great Depression of the 1930s. All across America, fortunes were lost and millions became jobless. In Chicago, where unemployment climbed above the national rate of 25 percent, more than 160 banks failed, and hundreds of families were evicted from their homes. But at least in 1933, people could look beyond the harsh realities of the day by escaping into the fantasy world of the "Century of Progress" World's Fair which opened that spring along Chicago's lakefront. Built on Northerly Island and filled-in land between 12th and 39th Streets, the fair commemorated Chicago's first 100 years and drew people from all over the world. Each day, more than 100,000 attended the exposition, whose theme was progress, both Chicago's and the world's at large. The fair's many colorful art deco buildings showcased everything modern, from large novel sculptures to advances in science, technology, communication, industry, transportation, and medicine, along with architectural visions of the future. Of equal attraction was Sally Rand, a buxom blonde burlesque dancer who drew crowds whenever she performed her risqué and well advertised "fan dance."

Despite the diversion of the Century of Progress, hardships brought by the Depression remained deeply entrenched in Chicago: the city was bankrupt, children were starving, and adults were jobless. As personal incomes disappeared or greatly diminished, tax bills went unpaid. Chicago's police officers and firefighters experienced barren paydays, receiving IOUs in place of paychecks. All across the country, financially-strapped cities were forced to disband fire companies and close fire stations. Chicago was no exception.

In the spring of 1934, during the fair's second season, Chicago was suffering from an extreme drought. Nowhere was the danger of a major fire more apparent than in the Union Stockyards on Chicago's south side. From a fire protection standpoint, the stockyards were a nightmare. Since it opened in 1865, the mile-square complex, with its wooden livestock pens, slaughterhouses, meatpacking plants, hay sheds, chemical laboratories, and railroad facilities had seen plenty of deadly fires. The worst was the December 22, 1910, Nelson-Morris fire that killed 21 firefighters and three workers. The conditions of early 1934 would help the stockyards and Packingtown make fire history again, and not since the Great

Scene showing the destruction wrought by the fire that raced through the stockyards and threatened the entire south side in 1934.

Fire of 1871 would Chicago firefighters be faced with the formidable task of saving their city from a major conflagration.

By Saturday May 15, 1934, rain had not fallen in weeks. The wooden livestock pens and hay sheds in the stockyards were bone dry, making an already dangerous fire hazard even worse. Just about everything in the stockyards was made of wood. Thousands of feet of lumber had been used to build the pens, sheds, and storage shanties as well as the miles of enclosed double-deck runways used to route the animals to the killing floors. Although several permanent buildings had been built of fire resistive materials, none was sprinklered, including the large Stockyards Exchange Building, where all business and futures trading occurred. To help minimize the hazards, two fire companies were stationed there, Engines 53 and 59, while several others were located in nearby neighborhoods. Nevertheless, access and mobility inside the vast complex was severe-

ly limited by the elaborate maze of narrow wooden runways, alleys, and gates, making the positioning of fire apparatus difficult. Fire hydrants were spread great distances apart, and the water mains servicing the area were too small to supply an adequate flow necessary to fight a large and sustained fire. These factors would play a significant role in the holocaust that was about to erupt.

Because it was a weekend, the slaughterhouses sat idle and empty save for a few watchmen and livestock workers. At 4:21 in the afternoon, a security guard saw flames and smoke coming from the cattle and sheep pens near 43rd and Morgan. Fanned by a 15-m.p.h. wind, the fire spread quickly, mainly in a northeasterly direction. The guard ran to his shanty and pulled a private A.D.T. fire alarm that was immediately routed to the fire department, and a box alarm assignment of four engines, two hook-and-ladders, a squad, a high-pressure rig, three chiefs, and several other units was then dispatched.

Engines 53 and 59 arrived in minutes, but already 300 square feet of pens were on fire, as well as the 43rd Street viaduct and the adjacent elevated chutes and cattle runs. After hooking up to a private fire hydrant, the two companies went to work on Texas Avenue, a narrow lane inside the pens near the fire's origin. Cowboys and cattle workers tried driving animals away from immediate danger, but the fire was jumping 50 to 100 feet at a time and sparking additional flames ahead. Water from the hoses turned to steam, and the fire surrounded the men, forcing them to drop their hoselines and flee for their lives. One cowboy was not so lucky. Along with several head of cattle, he became trapped and was cremated. The fire also destroyed all of the fire hose and both fire engines that had been abandoned.

Five minutes after the first call, Fourth Division Marshal John Costello sounded a 4-11 alarm from a city firebox in the stockyards, summoning 15 more engines, three hook-and-ladders, two water towers, two rescue companies, and two high-pressure rigs. Even with help on the way, the firefighters retreated two blocks further and attempted to set up a fire line near Engine 59's firehouse at Dexter and Exchange Avenues, half of a mile from where the fire started. But driven by strong winds, the fire "rushed at us with a scream and a roar as though especially bent on our total destruction," Chief Costello later recalled. "We dropped everything and ran, just barely getting away."[1] Everything in the fire's path was destroyed, including hundreds of head of livestock, thousands of feet of frame runway pens, and a huge supply of dry hay. Where cowboys couldn't drive animals to safety, police moved in and mercifully shot numerous cattle unable to escape.

Within minutes the firebox used to transmit the 4-11 alarm was destroyed. With ammonia tanks exploding in burning meatpacking houses, fire officers sent a 5-11 alarm at 4:35 P.M. before abandoning Engine 59's building, which lay directly in the fire's path. It was quickly destroyed along with all of the equipment inside. Conditions grew steadily worse as the hot wind spurred strong gales that blew up to 60 m.p.h. The blaze was now a firestorm leaping from building to building, principally in a northeasterly direction.

Special calls went out summoning fire companies from all over Chicago. Suburban fire departments also sent equipment to cover empty city firehouses. As more equipment arrived, firefighters attempted another stand east of the fire, but this position also had to be abandoned. The huge wall of flame continued to raze frame and brick buildings, including sheds and small warehouses loaded with combustibles, several two-story brick horse barns, and the three-story South Exchange Building. As the fire spread further east, it took over the nine-story main Exchange Building, where one of the most

dramatic rescues in Chicago history occurred.

At 5:15 P.M., firefighters saw four men on the roof of the Exchange Building waving for help. Sensing that the workers were ready to jump, the firemen positioned Hook-and-Ladder 4 next to the burning structure and raised the rig's 85-foot aerial ladder. The ladder, however, fell short of the roof, reaching only within three feet of an eighth-floor window.

Halsted Street's fire-ravaged business district.

Time was running out, and with heat and smoke pouring from all windows of the doomed building, Lieutenant Thomas Morrissey and three firefighters, John Tebbens, Joseph Reszal, and Robert Quinn (later to become Chicago's fire commissioner), raced up the wooden aerial carrying rope and a pompier ladder. Morrissey entered an eighth-floor window and hooked the pompier ladder to the edge of the roof, enabling the other three firefighters to climb the remaining distance and grab the trapped workers. Firefighters below held a life net as enginemen shot a protective stream of water toward the tenuous perch above. After bringing the workers down, the firefighters had to retreat further east to keep ahead of the main fire.

The U.S. Post Office sent 15 trucks to retrieve mail from the stockyards postal station before fire destroyed the building. Hundreds of families had to abandon their homes, while underground tanks of neighborhood gas stations were emptied of fuel and trucked away. Armored cars took away cash from the Drovers Exchange National Bank; however, money was left at the Livestock National Bank, because its vaults were considered fire resistant. Police cordoned off a three-square-mile area, the largest fire line in Chicago since the Great Fire of 1871, from 31st Street south to 55th Street and from Wentworth Avenue west to Ashland Avenue. By 5:30 P.M., the fire had swept the entire eastern portion of the yards, from Racine Avenue east to Halsted Street and from 41st Street south to 47th Street. Inside the affected area, residents helped firemen couple hoses together and push cars out of the way. Heat from the fire peeled paint off many of the vehicles. At 6 P.M. many buildings that lay in the fire's path were dynamited. The fourteenth special call was sounded at 6:32 P.M., and at the direction of Chief Fire Marshal Michael Corrigan, a third and final stand was mounted along Halsted Street between 40th and 43rd Streets in the form of a

Gutted Exchange Building, where firefighters rescued workers trapped on the roof.

semi-circle, which proved effective. Water supplying the fire line now came from city mains outside the stockyards, a source far superior to the diminished flow of the private hydrants inside the yards. Deploying high caliber turret streams fixed to squad trucks, high-pressure wagons, and water towers, the firefighters finally blocked the fire's advance, but not before a string of brick and frame commercial structures along Halsted Street had been incinerated, including two banks, a bowling alley, several restaurants, and a drug store, as well as most of the buildings in the Exchange-Halsted corridor. At one point the fire jumped Halsted Street and extended one block east to the Canaryville neighborhood, following a path along Emerald Avenue between Root and 43rd Streets. Another blaze caused by flying embers broke out in a vacant factory 900 feet south of the main fire, at 39th Street and Union Avenue. Fire companies quickly doused the fire before it could spread further.

As dusk arrived, the wind shifted south and the fire began losing momentum. After backtracking and burning several more buildings it had initially passed over, the fire ran out of fuel. The winds subsided, and by 11 P.M. the fire was deemed under control. It wasn't until the following day, Sunday, May 16, however, some 31 hours after the first alarm, that Chief Corrigan finally declared it "struck out."

Damage was incredible, and even before the smoke had cleared, people began referring to the stockyards fire as the second great Chicago fire. Dozens of buildings and more than 50 acres of livestock pens had been lost. Eight square city blocks were destroyed with total property losses exceeding $6 million, $5 million of which was covered by insurance. About 150 families were left homeless. The interior and contents of the Stock Yards Inn and the Breeding Building were demolished, the structures themselves severely damaged. Also lost was the 150,000-square-foot Stock Pavilion between Dexter Park Avenue and the east side of Halsted Street. (The pavilion was quickly rebuilt and renamed the International Amphitheater. In 1999, the famed building, probably best known for hosting the ill-fated 1968 Democratic National Convention, was razed.)

Miraculously only one person was killed, the cattle worker who had died in the early stages. About 800 to 1,000 head of livestock were lost. The 1933 grand-champion bull, Highland Stamp, was

One of several fire engines destroyed in the blaze.

rescued, along with eight prize cows and two other bulls taken from the Stock Pavilion by the arena's caretaker and a 12-year-old neighborhood boy who corralled the animals in a playground just beyond the fire area. Fifty-four firefighters had been injured, and another 26 became sick after drinking contaminated water from cattle troughs. About 126 men received preventative typhoid inoculations. A total force of 1,600 firefighters fought the fire, including the entire off-duty shift. Together they operated 100 engines, 12 hook-and-ladders, three squads, and numerous other pieces of special apparatus and equipment, a response equal to 19 alarms, clearly making this one of Chicago's biggest fires. Suburban fire departments that had sent equipment to cover empty Chicago fire stations handled 15 other fires inside the city.

Along with Engine 59's 1880 firehouse, six fire engines, one hook-and-ladder truck, and one water tower were either damaged or destroyed. Two of the rigs, Engines 59 and 98, both Ahrens-Foxes, were later rebuilt and returned to service. Also burned were 35,000 feet of fire hose and numerous pieces of equipment and hose appliances. How the fire started was never officially determined, but it is suspected that a cigarette or a match was tossed into a haystack inside the cattle and sheep pens near 43rd and Morgan Streets where the fire was discovered. Another theory suggests a spark may have come from a car driving on the 43rd Street overpass above the pens. Arson was never ruled out, but because of the extent of the damage in the area of origin, a definitive cause could never be established.

View of the gutted lobby and mezzanine of the LaSalle Hotel, sight of Chicago's worst hotel fire.

LaSalle Hotel Fire

The year 1946 was a bad one for hotel fires in the United States. In a span of just six months, three occurring in the month of June alone, deadly overnight fires broke out in four hotels, killing 228 people, including two firefighters. On June 19, fire killed 19 people at the Canfield Hotel in Dubuque, Iowa. Two days later, ten guests died in a fire at Dallas's Baker Hotel. Then, on December 7, the country experienced its worst hotel fire when the Winecoff Hotel in Atlanta burned, claiming 119 lives. Perhaps some of these deaths might have been averted if lessons had been heeded following the loss of 61 people on June 5, 1946, in an early morning fire at the LaSalle Hotel in downtown Chicago.

When it opened in 1909 at the corner of LaSalle and Madison Streets near the hub of Chicago's financial district, the 23-story LaSalle was called the "largest, safest and most modern hotel west of New York City."[1] Luxury abounded in the hotel's stately interior: its ornate walnut-paneled lobby and magnificent rooftop garden made it one of the city's most fashionable venues, a place to see and be seen. From the beginning the LaSalle ranked as a favorite of the elite; Mrs. Potter Palmer and other society divas often dined or held court in its lavish Blue Fountain Room, and for many years, the Illinois Republican Party maintained its headquarters there. During one extended visit to Chicago, President William Howard Taft conducted affairs of state from the hotel, turning the third-floor presidential suite into an ex-officio White House. But missing from the LaSalle was the means to detect and suppress a fire, a situation that ultimately brought the hotel another type of lasting fame. Though not as readily noticeable from a fire protection standpoint, the LaSalle Hotel was as dangerous as any skid row flophouse, and its place in history would be assured as the site of Chicago's fourth deadliest blaze and America's third worst hotel fire.

At midnight June 5, 1946, there were 1,059 registered patrons occupying the hotel's 886 rooms. Another 108 employees were on duty. Guests considered themselves fortunate because Chicago was still in the grip of a post-war housing shortage. Most hotel rooms continued to be rationed, and guests were allowed lodging only for two or three days.

A few night owls were nursing drinks inside the LaSalle's ground-floor Silver Grill Cocktail Lounge when, at around 12:20 A.M., someone smelled wood burning. Seconds later smoke and a little flame shot up from beneath the paneling along the lounge's south wall. Rather than notify the fire department, an ex-marine and several hotel employees tried extinguishing what they thought was a small fire by squirting a bottle of seltzer water at it and throwing sand. But when a large sheet of fire burst through the wall and across the combustible ceiling, their miscalculation became apparent and the fate of the LaSalle was sealed.[2]

With no sprinkler system to impede its progress, the fire quickly grew and completely enveloped the cocktail lounge, forcing the occupants to flee. In no time the fire spread beyond the cocktail lounge into the the two-story, wood-paneled lobby— feeding on a plentiful supply of combustible materials that included rugs, furniture, highly varnished walnut paneling, and acoustic ceiling tile—and into the mezzanine level through several large openings overlooking the lobby. So rapidly did the fire spread throughout the ground floor of the supposedly fireproof hotel that two cashiers working in the opposite end of the lobby were killed when they momentarily delayed their escape to gather up valuables.

The fire traveled quickly to the upper residential floors via the two open staircases in the middle of the lobby and the two central elevator shafts. Ringing telephones and cries of help alerted the unsuspecting guests, who upon opening their doors were met by a wall of smoke. Many became disoriented or panicked and ran into the corridors where they inhaled the toxic smoke, collapsed, and died. Smoke was also drawn into guestrooms with open glass transoms, resulting in further deaths.

As much as 15 minutes elapsed before someone telephoned the fire department. Finally, at 12:35 A.M., the main fire alarm office in City Hall received the first fire report. A still alarm was transmitted to nearby Engine 40, Hook-and-Ladder 6,

Squad 1, and the chief of the 1st battalion. A fire patrol squad was also assigned. When Battalion Chief Eugene Freeman pulled up two minutes later, he found the entire first floor and mezzanine engulfed in flames. The 49-year-old Freeman was no stranger to calamity, having returned to the fire department the previous October after serving two years as a naval lieutenant, where he had been decorated for heroism. He encountered a large number of hotel guests hanging out open windows, calling for help and tossing out lamps and other objects to draw attention. Some had even knotted bed sheets together and hung them out the windows.

With time running against him because of the delay in notification, Freeman ordered Engine 40 to drop two hoselines in front of the hotel's main entrance and begin fighting the fire from the outside. Truck 6 raised its 85-foot aerial ladder while other firefighters from Squad 1 and the fire patrol used ground ladders to reach guests at the second- and third-story windows. Several at the lower story windows were rescued, but those above the fourth floor remained beyond reach. Seeing the enormity of the situation, Freeman had his driver run to the nearest fire alarm box 200 feet south of the hotel to transmit a second alarm. (Fire companies were not yet equipped with two-way radios in 1946; only three fire units in the entire Chicago Fire Department had them.) The alarm was received at 12:39 A.M., and six minutes later, First Division Marshal Gibbons requested additional help by transmitting a 5-11 alarm, quickly followed by six more special alarms summoning a force of 61 fire companies and 300 firefighters.

As more engine companies arrived, firefighters stretched 15 hoselines into the lobby. Another 17 hoselines were dragged up ladders and the hotel's two fire escapes to fight flames between floors two through seven. Firefighters also used 23 hoselines supplied by the building's standpipe system to extinguish the

Crowds gather amid fire apparatus parked outside the LaSalle Street entrance of the LaSalle Hotel.

fires burning in the two central elevator shafts and in the hotel's penthouse.

Firefighters worked in the lobby while others cooled them off with another hose stream from behind. As the fire lessened, Freeman led firefighters into the foyer area to search for victims. Suddenly a large section of the mezzanine collapsed and trapped the rescuers. Firefighters working outside ran into the building and dug out 30 of their comrades. Though freed, Freeman was critically injured and later died in the hospital from smoke inhalation.

Following the collapse, it took firefighters about 30 minutes to conquer the fire in the lobby, but considerably longer to succeed on the floors above. The dying and dead were lying everywhere, most overcome by smoke. Fire Commissioner Michael Corrigan brought in personnel and life-saving equipment and ordered a search of every room in the building. In their uphill attempts to revive the unconscious victims, rescuers relied on resuscitators or artificial respiration, reportedly saving 50 lives. Fire company reports also indicate that more than 150 others were rescued from the lower seven floors by ladders, while another 900 were led to safety down the two outside fire escapes that emptied into the alley.

Most guests who remained calm escaped with their lives. One couple barricaded themselves in their 18th floor room and stuck their heads out the bathroom window to breathe clean air until firefighters arrived. A *Chicago Tribune* reporter who had just returned from China and his wife wrapped their faces in wet towels and groped through smoke before reaching a nearby fire escape.[3] Staffers and guests also felt their way through

The charred walls and ceiling of the LaSalle Hotel's third floor corridor.
It was on this floor where the majority of the 61 victims had been trapped.

the smoky corridors and helped at least 27 to safety, among them a legless amputee. Perhaps the most dramatic escape was made by a 23-year-old blind woman from El Paso, who, after donning her robe and slippers, calmly followed her seeing eye dog to a window and then down a fire escape.

A first-aid station and temporary morgue was set up in Chicago City Hall two blocks north on LaSalle Street, where more than 200 received medical attention and where the sheet-covered bodies of 42 of the 61 men, women, and children who died in the fire were laid out in neat rows. Most died or were injured from smoke inhalation. Contrary to initial reports, there was no evidence of severe injury or death from falls from upper floors. Seven bodies—a man, his wife, and their 4-year-old daughter among them—were found on the small court roof above the mezzanine. It is believed these people escaped through adjoining windows but died from the smoke. Of the 61 victims, 50 had died at the scene, losing their lives within 15 minutes of the fire's discovery. Another nine were dead on arrival at nearby emergency rooms, while the remaining two died later in hospitals.

The dead had varied backgrounds. They included 41-year-old Julia Barry, a night telephone operator at the hotel. A widow, she was the mother of a 16-year-old son and had spent the past 11 years working at the LaSalle. She died at her switchboard on the second-floor while attempting to wake up sleeping guests. Also killed were five Iowa teenagers who had been given a trip to Chicago as a graduation present by their parents, and the mayor and three other public officials from downstate Quincy, Illinois. They were in Chicago to meet with federal housing officials about providing temporary housing for returning war veterans. The four were to stay at the nearby Bismarck Hotel but changed to the LaSalle due to a last-minute reservation mix-up. The day after the fire, a jury awarded a widow killed in the blaze $1 million in a civil lawsuit she had been pursuing for 17 years regarding assets from her late husband's company. The award was bequeathed to a nephew.

Investigators sifting through the ruins the next day were unable to determine exactly how the fire started, but they did pinpoint its origin to a specific concealed wallspace in the Silver Grill Cocktail Lounge adjacent to the LaSalle Street lobby entrance. Investigators put forward the theory that a cigarette may have been tossed into the elevator shaft next to the cocktail lounge, landing in the concealed wall space between the lounge and the lobby. Another possibility was that an overheated ceiling light in the lounge may have ignited the combustible wooden joists in the ceiling, or that a short circuit in improperly-ducted wiring behind the wall sparked the fire. Suspicion that a leaky natural gas line may have played a role was ruled out after a thorough inspection of the utilities.

Further examination revealed the marked absence of an automatic sprinkler system, suitable fire detection system (i.e., smoke and heat detectors), and an audible fire alarm. Had such measures been in place, the fire could have easily been discovered during its incipient stage, triggering an alarm that would have alerted the occupants and the fire department. The use of combustible materials in the lobby and mezzanine also played a key role in the disaster. The presence of these materials was akin to erecting a two-story combustible building in the elegant hotel lobby. The ornate paneling created a major fire hazard in a building that otherwise featured fire-resistive construction. The paneling had been installed on a frame of wooden furring strips that created concealed spaces inside the walls. The fire burned unnoticed here as well as in other hidden voids inside the dropped ceiling. Conditions were made worse because the many coats of lacquer and varnish on the paneling burst into flames just as if gasoline had been poured on them, explaining why it only took seconds before the lobby literally exploded. The combustible materials used to construct the Silver Grill Cocktail Lounge in 1934 violated the city's building code at the time.

The hotel had two main open stairways in the lobby next to the two banks of passenger elevators that serviced all 23 floors. Two other open stairways ran from the lobby to the second floor, while a third pair of stairways originated at the mezzanine level and extended up to the top floor. Although these latter two stairways had originally been enclosed, the doors had been removed at the mezzanine floor so that at the time of the fire they, like the others, could not be used for escape when they filled with smoke and fire. The building's two fire escapes led to the alley behind the hotel. Although the hotel's early plans had called for the installation of fire doors in the corridor at each stairway landing, the doors were deleted. Their presence could have saved many lives.

The LaSalle tragedy was important to fire protection specialists because of the extensive physical damage and high loss of life incurred in a structure considered fireproof. Recommendations made in the wake of the disaster included automatic sprinkler systems for hotels; installation of fire alarm detection systems linked to a central receiving station; and fire alarm boxes outside hotel lobbies. Also recommended were fire-resistive construction for hotels; enclosure of all vertical openings such as stairways and elevator shafts; installation of fire walls to subdivide large open areas; and elimination of hollow wooden walls, concealed wall spaces, and lacquered paneling. Frequent fire safety education sessions and fire drills for hotel employees were urged, too, with specific instructions directing employees to call the fire department whenever a fire is first discovered. A special mayoral committee also proposed that instructions be posted in all hotel rooms telling guests what to do in case of fire and describing escape routes. It was further recommended that all fire trucks be fitted with two-way radios.

Following a $2 million post-fire restoration, the LaSalle reopened in July 1947 and lived on for another 29 years. The Silver Grill Cocktail Lounge was also rebuilt and renamed The Hour Glass. In 1976, the hotel was sold to developers who razed it and built an indiscreet white office tower. No marker commemorates the 61 who lost their lives in the 1946 fire.

The scene following the collision of a streetcar and a gasoline truck at 62nd and State Streets. The May 25, 1950, crash killed 34 people and injured 50 more.

Streetcar Named Disaster

During the first half of the twentieth century, the streetcar had become a familiar sight in Chicago. As public conveyances, the trolleys made their debut in 1859, when horses pulled the first covered models over wooden and cobblestone streets. By the 1890s, electricity had taken the place of horses, making the clanging of bells and the bumping of wheels over steel tracks familiar and frequent sounds in many Chicago neighborhoods. So popular was their use that for a time, during the First World War, Chicago operated the largest streetcar system in the country. But as convenient and reliable as streetcars were for the thousands of loyal riders who relied on them daily, they did have their drawbacks. One obvious limitation was a lack of maneuverability and the fact that they couldn't detour around accidents, fires, or floods, setting the stage for one of the worst transportation mishaps in Chicago's history, and one of its most notorious fires.

On the fateful Thursday afternoon of May 25, 1950, a Green Hornet streetcar traveled south from the Loop through the slums along the south State Street line. Driving the streetcar was Paul J. Manning, a 42-year-old motorman who had been involved in at least ten minor streetcar accidents during his career with the CTA. A heavy spring thunderstorm the night before had flooded several sections along the State Street line, including the low underpass at 63rd Street, making the way impassable for electric streetcars. Consequently, CTA flagmen had spent most of that day detouring all southbound trolleys into a turnaround on the east side of State Street approximately one block north of the flooded viaduct. As a result, 62nd Street had become the temporary end of the line.

At 6:34 P.M., Manning was driving his Green Hornet at a speed estimated at 35 m.p.h., dangerously fast for the wet conditions ahead. The CTA flagman on duty was standing alongside the tracks at 62nd Place, one block north of the turnaround, when Manning's streetcar came into view. As it fast approached his position, the flagman waved his signal to warn the motorman to slow down and stop. But instead of slowing, the streetcar kept speeding with no sign of stopping. The flagman began waving more frantically as he attempted to warn the driver that a switch in the track was open for a turn that would put him directly in the path of oncoming northbound traffic. Included in that traffic was a tanker truck

The horrible sight of charred remains bunched up behind doors that failed to open.

into the tanker. The impact sliced open the tanker's steel skin, causing an enormous shower of sparks that ignited the spilling gasoline, incinerating Manning and 32 passengers on the spot.

The ensuing explosion rocked the entire neighborhood, and the burning gasoline overtook seven neighboring buildings. So hot was the petroleum-based fire that it twisted steel, fused and cracked windows, and melted sections of asphalt on the street. The walls of several buildings collapsed, though the occupants escaped safely. Drivers and passengers of automobiles lined up in traffic also managed to escape. Thirty people, however, did sustain injuries, some with serious burns.

loaded with 8,000 gallons of gasoline destined for numerous Chicago service stations.

Whether Manning failed to see the flagman's warning remains a mystery. What is known is that once the Green Hornet hit the open switch track, it swung suddenly left into the turn, violently jerking passengers to the floor. Manning was last seen throwing up his arms and screaming in horror as his streetcar careened through the intersection and plowed directly

Four alarms brought 30 fire companies to the scene. A little more than two hours passed before the worst of the flames were brought under control. But it would be a long time before a sense of calm revisited the area. Newspapers reported that as many as 20,000 people lined the streets to witness the fire. Steel safety bars intended to keep riders from sticking their heads and arms out the car prevented some passengers from escaping through the side windows.

When firefighters forced open the trolley's rear doors they were met with a ghastly scene: "In some cases we only found the skulls and parts of the limbs," recalled Fire Marshal Albert Peterson. "We had to remove all of them and make a temporary morgue on the sidewalk."[1]

Several riders escaped thanks to a 14-year-old girl who, while seated in the middle of the car, immediately pulled down on a red safety knob that opened the center doors. Unfortunately the rear doors were fitted with no such device; the so-called "blinker doors" were designed solely as entryways, and didn't open from inside, creating a bottle-neck for passengers trying to use this blocked route. When firefighters tore the doors open, they found a pile of charred bodies fused together.

A firefighter peers into the streetcar's scorched interior.

blackened streetcar.

The subsequent investigation revealed that the Green Hornet was in perfect working order, as was the gasoline truck. Like motorman Manning, the truck driver, Melvin Wilson, had also burned to death. But it was Manning who was held responsible for the accident, despite his defender's claims that he was simply following a CTA policy that placed greater emphasis on maintaining schedules rather than safety. Several flaws in the design of the Green Hornet also contributed to the death toll, including a lack of safety latches that would have provided an emergency escape route through the windows if there were no steel bars blocking the way. Window escape hatches were installed on all CTA vehicles, and steel bars were ordered removed from all trains and streetcars.

In a decision that was still being discussed in journalism ethics classes decades later, the city's newspapers, the *Chicago Herald-American* in particular, published graphic photos the next day showing the cremated bodies still piled up in the

In the years following the crash, streetcars began to slowly disappear from Chicago's main thoroughfares, replaced by busses. On June 21, 1958, the final run of a Green Hornet streetcar was made on Vincennes Avenue, closing another chapter in Chicago's history of fire tragedy.

A priest administers last rights to victims of the 1950 streetcar disaster.

Gutted remains of the Boston Hotel, 844 W. Madison St., where five men died in a fire October 12, 1953.
The Boston was typical of the squalid, unsafe flophouses that fronted much of Chicago's former skid row.

No Vacancy

Almost every city in America had a skid row. In New York it was the Bowery, in San Francisco the Mission District. For generations of Chicagoans, Madison Street defined the stereotypical image of alcoholism in America: a homeless drunk in a gutter, bereft of family and friends, jobless and destitute. Until its demise in the late 1970s, the west Madison skid row reigned as the epicenter of Chicago's seedy dark side. Though now a memory, its gauntlet of misery consisted largely of dingy saloons, greasy-spoon diners, storefront missions, and cheap hotels. Thievery, prostitution, and the dispensing of cheap booze were its main industries.

Mostly it was men who lived on skid row. They had few possessions and stayed mainly in local transient hotels that charged anywhere from 50 cents to $1 per "flop," and whose small "rooms" were often nothing more than caged mattresses partitioned by corrugated sheet metal walls and topped with wire mesh ceilings. Despite these crude and inhumane accommodations, they did manage to offer boarders at least some degree of sanctuary from the squalor of the street. But from a fire protection standpoint, these lodgings were unsafe, the danger manifested by a combination of factors that included overcrowding, combustible interior construction, open stairways, faulty wiring, poor housekeeping, and a marked absence of fire safety devices such as sprinkler systems, fire doors, and smoke alarms. These problems were finally brought to light following a series of fatal flophouse fires in the mid-1950s.

The deadly trend began March 20, 1953, when four people died in a fire at the four-story Chestnut Hotel near Rush Street. Later that year, on October 12, flames swept the Boston Hotel at 844 W. Madison St. in the heart of skid row, killing five. Then, on December 17, 1953, one resident and five firefighters lost their lives in an overnight fire that swept through the dilapidated Reliance Hotel at 1700 W. Madison St. Taken together, these fires awakened the public to the hazards of housing people in firetraps, even if those directly affected were considered societal misfits. A greater stir was created after 51 more people died in another string of hotel fires in 1955, prompting newspaper editorials that urged a crackdown by city fire inspectors and others to ensure that such tragedies were not repeated.

The worst of these deadly 1955 fires erupted February 12,

when 29 men died after flames gutted the five-story Barton Hotel at 644 W. Madison St. On the night in question, 245 men were reportedly staying inside the 49-year-old building, each having paid 65 cents for the privilege of a night's stay in one of its 336 "rooms," cubicles measuring four feet wide by six feet long and topped by seven-foot-high chicken-wire ceilings. At around 2 o'clock on that frigid Saturday morning, Tony Dykes, the hotel's night manager, was keeping warm by sitting close to the radiator in the Barton's second-floor office. A furniture fixture store occupied the first floor while the hotel took up the top four floors. Hearing a commotion down the hall, Dykes reportedly got up from his chair to see what was wrong. Seconds later, he was confronted by a human torch in the hallway, his hair, clothing, and body completely aflame. As smoke and flames poured from the open door of the burning man's room, Dykes hastened back to his office to pull the building's fire alarm, then returned to the corridor in a determined but hopeless attempt to bang on doors and arouse the sleeping tenants.

"Get up," Dykes yelled over the gong of the fire bell. "The whole place is on fire."[1] But because they had passed out in bed after a night of drinking in neighborhood saloons, many inhabitants remained oblivious to the danger. Still, Dykes made as much noise as he could before being driven from the building by the searing heat and blinding smoke.

Firefighters advance hose up the front fire escape of the doomed Barton Hotel at 644 W. Madison St. Another rescuer assists a resident down a ladder.

The fire spread quickly, invading the upper floors via an

open wooden stairway in back of the building. Flames blocked escape as thick smoke darkened the hallways. Several men opened their doors to flee, but after breathing in the superheated air and deadly gases, they fell to the floor unconscious and burned to death. Luckier residents reached the front fire escape and climbed down to safety. Others were forced to break windows and jump from ledges three and four stories high. At least one man slid down a rope used to lower garbage.

The first-arriving firefighters found a too-familiar scene: desperate men hanging from smoke-filled windows calling for rescue as fire roared behind them. Extra alarms were sounded as firefighters threw up ladders and deployed heavy water streams on the hotel's top floors. Intense flames and subzero temperatures made the firefighters' difficult job even worse. Many inhabitants fled the building in their underwear to a neighboring Salvation Army shelter, where clothing, food, and hot coffee waited. A few avoided death simply because they were away when the fire broke out, either in nearby taverns or locked up in the Des Plaines Street police station for public drunkenness. Some of the 29 dead were burned beyond recognition, and though fingerprint checks were made on the bodies, because most of the victims had been derelict and lacked proper identification, they died as they lived, nameless and unclaimed.

Firefighters remove one of 29 killed in the Barton Hotel fire, one of Chicago's worst flophouse blazes.

Officials attributed the cause of the Barton fire to a 70-year-old man who, while trying to massage his sore legs, had accidentally dropped a lit cigarette into a solution of rubbing alcohol, sparking a flash fire that ignited his body and the contents of his room.

Two months later, on April 28, 1955, Chicago awoke to another fire tragedy involving a transient hotel. This time eight men and three firefighters died in a four-alarm fire at the Green Mill Hotel at 518 N.

Green St., an older brick building that, like earlier scenarios, featured a combustible interior, open stairways, and no sprinkler system. The blaze erupted just after midnight, when many of the hotel's 85 residents were asleep. Flames originated

Exterior of the gutted Barton Hotel.

beneath a staircase on the first floor and spread so quickly that, by the time the first firefighters arrived, they were already exploding out the rear windows. Some 35 residents, including several women and children, hanging from the front windows were taken down with ground ladders. In the back of the building a father dangled his two small children from a fourth-floor bay window while his wife stood next to him clutching a third child. As smoke billowed from the window, firefighter Karl Scheel of Truck 14 shouted to them not to jump. Scheel climbed up a drainpipe to the second-story roof of an adjacent building, putting him directly beneath the trapped family. "Throw me the kids," he yelled to the parents who dropped them in his outstretched arms.[2] Firefighters then threw a ladder up to Scheel, who wedged it against the bay window and climbed up to rescue the mother. By this time smoke had overcome the husband and he fell back into the room unconscious. With flames searing his eyebrows, the determined Scheel reached over the sill, pulled the father up, threw his limp body over his shoulders and brought him down the ladder. For this rescue Scheel was awarded the fire department's highest award, the Carter Harrison Medal.

As the fire continued to burn, an interior stairway between the second and third floor collapsed, plunging several firefighters advancing a hoseline into the flames. One captain was killed instantly while a second firefighter died four days later. A deputy fire marshal suffered a heart attack and succumbed the following week. Another firefighter was burned over 75 percent of his body after being trapped in the collapse. He remained in a coma for two months while undergoing numerous skin grafts to rebuild his face, shoulders, and ears. Though he recovered, he never returned to work. Because the Green Mill fire was listed as suspicious, the 11 deaths resulting from it were ruled homicides. No arsonist was ever apprehended, and the case remains unsolved.

Just one week later, as the city still mourned the Green Mill tragedy, flames swept another hotel on skid row, the Comfort Inn at 919 W. Madison St., a five-story flophouse whose rates ranged between 70 cents a night to $8 per week.

The Comfort Inn was anything but comfortable; it contained 116 cubicles that, like so many other hotels, was partitioned by sheet metal walls and topped with chicken wire. The second floor held 26 of these so-called rooms while the three upper floors each held 30. A tavern occupied the building's first floor. The fire began around 1 A.M. on May 6, 1955, originating in a room on the second floor, possibly ignited when the occupant, who died in the blaze, either fell asleep or passed out while smoking in bed.

After the initial alarm, two police officers arrived first, and running into the burning building saved as many as 25 residents by guiding them through the smoke. Several more occupants were brought down fire department ladders by firefighters who were veterans of previous skid row fires; they were accustomed to the sight of raggedy derelicts hanging from hotel windows and screaming for help. In some instances, the firefighters had to fight numerous drunken residents who either panicked or turned belligerent and tried running back inside the burning building. Several other occupants either balked from fright or refused to get out of bed and resisted firefighters searching their smoke-filled rooms. Rescuers had no choice but to drag them to ladders or to the rear fire escape and force them down. Because of the enormous life safety hazard and rescue work involved, the fire was elevated to three alarms. But even though the fire was put out in 47 minutes, the flames and smoke had killed ten residents and sent 20 more to hospitals with severe burns and injuries.

Following the Comfort Inn fire, Chicago Mayor Richard J.

Daley vowed to tear down every remaining skid row hotel and replace them with modern buildings. Though it took two decades to accomplish, Daley did make true on the promise. Construction of a central expressway system in the late 1950s helped mitigate some of the slums along Madison Street. Further urban renewal and reconstruction efforts in the late 1970s and 1980s, as well as gentrification in the 1990s, transformed the entire area into one that today resembles none of its former self.

FOR A while it seemed that Chicago's run of fatal hotel fires had come to an end. But not so. On January 25, 1970, flames broke out again, not in a seedy flophouse, but the 31-story Conrad Hilton Hotel at 720 S. Michigan Ave. The Sunday morning fire erupted shortly before 7 A.M., as guests slept in the 2,600-unit luxury hotel. And though the fire was confined to the ninth floor, and in a building with the latest in fire safety equipment, two 18-year-old men, both deaf and mute, were killed. Another 38 guests were injured. The two victims had been among a group of 41 students with physical disabilities visiting Chicago from downstate Illinois.

Before the close of the twentieth century, Chicago would be hit with two more notable hotel fires, in 1981 and 1993. In each case, the buildings housed transient residents and were considerably lacking in fire safety.

In the roaring twenties, the Royal Beach Hotel had been a fashionable venue, home to young singles and married couples lured to the bright lights and bustle of Uptown. During the Jazz Age years, the densely-populated north side neighborhood was one of the largest retail and entertainment districts outside the Loop, boasting speakeasies, movie theaters, dance halls, and jazz joints. Among the better-known was the splendid Aragon

Firefighters work to extinguish a fire inside a bar along the Clark Street skid row in 1959.

ballroom on Lawrence Avenue and, just around the corner on Broadway, the famed Green Mill nightclub that had once been run by mobster Machine Gun Jack McGurn. Nightlife aside, Uptown had also served briefly as the center of the fledgling moving picture industry. Prior to 1918, before filmmakers moved to California, many movies were shot at the Essanay film studio on Argyle Street, including pictures starring Charlie Chaplin, Gloria Swanson, and Wallace Beery.

But the Depression years delivered hard times to Uptown, and as its allure faded, the once glamorous neighborhood became a forsaken transient district. After World War II, southern blacks, Appalachian whites, and Native Americans moved into the area, drawn by the cheap rents of an abundant stock of rooming houses, residence hotels, and apartment buildings. By 1981, Uptown rivaled that of any urban tenderloin: taverns, currency exchanges, and cut-rate stores lined its streets while its alleys and dark corners were frequented by pimps, prostitutes, thieves, and dope pushers. Uptown was also one of Chicago's most arson-plagued neighborhoods, many of the fires the result of insurance fraud schemes in which building owners hired professionals to burn down dilapidated structures and then collected large cash settlements. In 1979, six people lost their lives in one such apartment building fire.

The once stylish Royal Beach was not untouched by the downfall of Uptown. It had become just another apartment hotel. Though several elderly men and women on public aid lived there, it was also home to recovering alcoholics, drug addicts, prostitutes, the unemployed, and the mentally ill.

On March 14, 1981, residents were still asleep in the hotel at 5523 N. Kenmore when smoke began to fill the hallways at 3 A.M. Someone finally noticed it and started screaming, alerting the residents. By the time they realized what was happening, flames and smoke were spreading rapidly throughout the four-story hotel. Panic caused by the fire was heightened when the electricity failed, plunging the building into darkness, leaving occupants to grope their way through the smoke in search of an exit.

When the closest firefighters pulled up in front of the Royal Beach they went right to work, throwing up ladders to panicky residents hanging out windows. But as they scrambled to save those trapped inside, flames and smoke thwarted their efforts by cutting off escape for many tenants and forcing some to jump. After stretching hoselines through the building and positioning a snorkel in the alley next to the hotel, firefighters gained the upper hand by extinguishing the main body of fire. But when they conducted a room-by-room search, instead of survivors they found unconscious and lifeless bodies. Most of the victims had been asphyxiated by dense smoke. Nineteen were dead and 14 injured.

The cause of the fire was attributed not to the actions of any resident but to faulty electrical wiring in a first-floor laundry room. Fire officials also suspected that a second point of origin might have been in the rear stairwell, though this was never officially determined due to the extent of the damage. Investigators did reveal that the hotel's management had been in and out of housing court for numerous building code violations. The Royal Beach had no sprinkler system, and because smoke detectors in the building reportedly failed to operate, many occupants were unaware of the fire until it was too late. As in previous hotel fires, some of the Royal Beach victims were never identified because they lacked proper identification and had no known family.

CHICAGO HISTORY would repeat itself in 1993, when 20 residents of the Paxton Hotel died in a suspicious fire whose circumstances were strikingly similar to the Royal Beach fire 12 years earlier. Like previous cases, tragedy came during the pre-dawn hours when flames erupted inside the single-room occupancy (SRO) hotel that lacked adequate fire protection and featured open stairways and no fire doors. But even as deadly as the Paxton fire was, extraordinary heroics by Chicago firefighters prevented it from becoming an even greater disaster.

Like the Royal Beach, the Paxton was a four-story building of ordinary construction: the facade of the 60-year-old hotel was brick but its interior was made of wood, plaster, and other combustible materials. Unlike the Royal Beach, the Paxton was located not in a shabby part of town but at 1432 N. LaSalle Street in trendy Old Town, near Lincoln Park and the Gold Coast. Despite this desirable locale, the Paxton Hotel was home to residents on fixed incomes, mainly students, the elderly, and those trying to make a new start in life. Rents for each of its

140 rooms averaged $90 a week, enabling its occupants the convenience of month-to-month living. To keep costs affordable for such people, the city of Chicago did not require owners of SRO hotels to install expensive safety features such as sprinkler systems. As benevolent as this gesture seemed, the end result was a much heavier price paid in lives.

At 4 A.M. March 16, 1993, the Paxton's estimated 160 residents were roused by screams, shouts, and the unmistakable smell of smoke. A fire that had originated in a rear stairwell was spreading rapidly throughout the hotel via the unenclosed stairway in the back of the building. Though it is not known who first noticed the fire, the first call reporting it to the fire department was logged at 4:05 A.M. In the next few minutes, five alarms plus numerous special calls for ambulances would be sounded, bringing much of Chicago's on-duty firefighting force to the scene.

When the first firefighters from Engine 4 and Tower Ladder 10 arrived at the yellow brick building, they saw dozens of residents hanging out windows as smoke billowed from behind. Some had already jumped and were lying on the sidewalk or in the alleyway next to the building. As residents opened their windows to escape, strong winds blew through the structure and fanned the flames. As the fire grew, occupants who opened their doors were forced back inside their rooms. With no other way out, they took to the window ledges and waited for ladders. The rapid spread of flames and smoke was aided by the removal of fire doors from stairway landings and hallways for remodeling and never replaced. A second source of fresh oxygen came from a back door that was left open.

These factors, together with 20- to 30-m.p.h. winds and a cold drizzle that kept the smoke from lifting, made firefighting

Scene outside the fire-wrecked Paxton Hotel, where 20 residents died in a pre-dawn blaze that struck the building on March 16, 1993.

very difficult. Nevertheless, rescuers scaled ladders placed against the front of the building and plucked dozens of residents from upper floors windows, lowering them one by one to the sidewalks and alley. The physical strain on the rescuers was enormous, but they continued to revive unconscious victims on the sidewalk, picking up others and carrying them to ambulances. Quick work by the fire department during those precious early minutes resulted in an estimated 70 lives being saved.

Eventually the intensity of the fire drove the firefighters from the building, and they were forced to set up ladder pipes and wage battle from the outside. After water was poured on the hotel for several hours, its wooden interior collapsed into the basement and the fire eventually burned itself out. But because several people were unaccounted for, rescuers used heavy equipment to knock down the walls and spent the next seven days scouring the ruins for the missing. Some turned up in hospitals or telephoned officials to let them know they were alive. But the whereabouts of a few others were left unknown. After a week of sifting the debris bucket by bucket, two more bodies were recovered. Finally, the search was terminated and the death toll ended at 20.

Like many big fires, the Paxton blaze remains a mystery largely because the extent of the destruction was so great that it made pinning down an exact cause difficult. Officials speculated that a frayed cord on a space heater in a first-floor room might have sparked it. Another theory said an unattended hot plate was responsible. As for life safety, though the Paxton was equipped with smoke detectors, it lacked an internal local fire alarm as well as any automatic means to alert the fire department to a fire. But because the city had chosen to ease building codes so operators of SRO hotels could keep their rates low, the hotel wasn't required to have such devices. It's no surprise that in the wake of the Paxton disaster, the city upgraded its SRO laws.

Avers Avenue in front of the north wing of Our Lady of the Angels school, where 95 died in the December 1, 1958, fire.

Legacy of the Angels

Fires are not supposed to happen, but when they do and people die, they can affect an entire community, especially if children are involved. Never was this more apparent than on December 1, 1958, when Chicago and the nation experienced one of the most heartbreaking tragedies in history. On that day a fire enveloped the half-century-old Our Lady of the Angels parochial school on Chicago's west side, leaving 92 students and three nuns dead.

To examine the school fire is to revisit a story filled with startling inconsistencies and shattering grief, a tale of ordinary people caught up in a mind-numbing disaster, the effects of which would still be felt decades later. Not only did this fire shock the world and tear apart a close-knit community, it left lingering questions that turned the event into a mystery that has deepened with each passing year.

What is known is that in the fall of 1958, classroom space at Our Lady of the Angels was strained to capacity, a dangerous situation present in hundreds of American elementary schools, public and private. Some 1,400 students, 20 nuns, and nine lay teachers occupied its 24 classrooms where, in some, up to 60 children were jammed together. The 2½-story brick school building on the corner of Avers Avenue and Iowa Street was the hub of a thriving Roman Catholic parish in a well-kept, predominantly Italian neighborhood. The U-shaped school consisted of a north and south wing connected by an annex. The south wing was built in 1903, and the north wing, which had originally been designed as a combination church-school, was built in 1910. In 1939, after a new church was built next door, the school's north wing was converted entirely into classrooms, and a chapel was built in its basement.

December 1, 1958, promised to be a cold but clear day in Chicago. For pupils at Our Lady of the Angels, it was the first day of class since school had let out the week before for Thanksgiving. The day passed without fanfare and everything seemed normal. At 2 P.M. the students settled down for their final hour of lessons, eagerly awaiting the three o'clock bell that would signal their dismissal. But lurking nearby was a hidden fire burning in the basement stairwell of the school's north wing. Exactly when it started was never fixed to the precise minute, but the date of its occurrence will never be forgotten. Because the school lacked an adequate fire detection system, several minutes would pass before anyone discovered the blaze.

Firefighters bring victims down from blazing classrooms in the alley north of the school.

Two boys returning to their second-floor classroom after emptying wastebaskets thought they smelled something burning. When they reached their room in the building's annex, they informed their teacher, who stepped into the hallway to find smoke gathering at ceiling level. After conferring with a neighboring teacher, she ran down to the principal's office in the school's south wing to seek direction. (A standing rule prohibited anyone from sounding the school's fire alarm without first notifying the mother superior.) After learning the principal was substituting in another classroom downstairs, the teacher hastened back to her own classroom, where the smoke in the hallway had thickened. Rather than wait for an alarm, she and the neighboring teacher promptly evacuated their children down a stairway to a set of exit doors in the south wing. After marching their pupils into the church next door, the first teacher ran back to the school and pulled the fire alarm while the other teacher took off for the convent across the street to use the telephone. The fire alarm started ringing in the school at 2:42 P.M., the same time the first telephone call reporting the fire was received by the fire department. For the 329 students and teachers in the north wing's second floor classrooms, the signal came too late. Flames and smoke had already traveled up the rear stairway and entered the long corridor, cutting off escape.

The unsuspecting occupants were first alerted to the fire not by the alarm but by a series of events that began with an ominous rising heat inside the building and the sound of doors rattling. In Room 208, next to burning stairway, children giggled when someone suggested "it must be ghosts." But the laughter stopped when a boy got up from his desk and opened the back door. "There's smoke in the hallway!" he exclaimed. Waiting for the fire alarm, Sister Mary St. Canice instructed her 46 seventh graders to stay seated and calm. "We mustn't panic," she told them. "Get down on your knees and pray. The firemen will come." The nun meant well. But her instructions were quickly abandoned by the will to survive. When glass transoms over the doors shattered, smoke and fire spilled into the room across the combustible ceiling tile, plunging it into superheated darkness. Chased by flames, the children rushed to the windows and began screaming "the school's on fire!" Seconds later the youngsters started jumping out the windows, bouncing off the pavement 25 feet below. Some broke bones and limped or crawled away. Others remained silent and still. Those unable to escape the room fell to the floor where they died. As the fire advanced further through the corridor, the same harrowing scene was repeated in each of the remaining five classrooms.[1]

As terror unfolded inside, those outside became aware of the fire. At around 2:30 P.M., janitor Jim Raymond had been walking between the narrow gangway separating the back of the school and parish rectory when he saw smoke and a red glow coming from one of the school's frosted basement window panes. Raymond ran into the rectory to get help. "The school's on fire!" he yelled to the housekeeper, Nora Maloney. "Call the fire department, quick!"[2] Raymond then disappeared back in the school, inside of which were four of his own children. Maloney's actions at this point remain unclear because her call, the first report to the fire department, wasn't received until 2:42 P.M. Meanwhile, after reentering the school basement, Raymond attempted to douse the flames himself. But the fire was too big for him to handle alone, so he ran up a set of stairs to the second floor where he was met by one of the parish priests. Together they helped evacuate a classroom next to the building's only fire escape. In the next few minutes, the janitor made several more trips before passing out.

About the same time Raymond discovered the fire, traveling

Another victim is removed down a ladder.

salesman Elmer Barkhaus was driving south on Avers Avenue when he too saw smoke coming from the school's northeast doorway that led to the basement and faced the alley directly north of the school. Barkhaus pulled his car over and, after finding no fire alarm box on the corner, ran into a small candy store next door to telephone. The store's owner, a Polish immigrant named Barbara Glowacki, was leery of strangers, so when the excited Barkhaus barged up to her front counter, she said she had "no public phone."[3]

"The school next door is on fire," Barkhaus yelled before running out the door to ring doorbells on neighboring homes. Glowacki went into the alley to investigate the stranger's report. She saw smoke and a wisp of flame shooting from the transom above the school's rear stairwell door. Fear shot through her body; her daughter Helena's classroom was on the first floor. She hurried back to the store and called the fire department. After being told that "help is on the way," Glowacki returned to the alley. This time she saw frantic students and nuns leaning out the upper windows. They were shrouded in black smoke that pushed from behind them. "Help us," they screamed, "We're trapped." But before Glowacki could react, the first of dozens of students began jumping the 25 feet to the icy pavement.

Sirens began to fill the neighborhood and harried parents and neighbors ran into the alley carrying painting ladders that fell far short of the window ledges. When Engine 85 pulled up, its crew saw smoke and flames surging from the school's upper windows and children dropping from the sills, many with their clothing and hair aflame. The fire was soon elevated to five alarms, bringing 60 fire companies and ambulances to the scene. Desperate as the situation was, in the decisive early moments of their arrival, firefighters still managed to save 160 children by pulling them out windows, passing them down ladders, catching them in life nets, or otherwise breaking their falls before they hit the ground. One rescuer who climbed a ladder to Room 211 was Lieutenant Charles Kamin of Hook-and-Ladder 35. When he reached the window, scores of 8th graders were bunched together trying to squeeze out. The fireman reached in and began grabbing the children one at a time, swinging them around his back and dropping them to the ladder. He didn't have time to worry if they missed. A broken bone from falling was better than dying. Kamin rescued about nine children, mostly boys because he could grab them by their belts. He was stopped when the room exploded in fire and the remaining pupils at the window fell back in the flames beyond his reach.

It took fire crews a little more than an hour to put out the fire. But when they entered the second-story classrooms in the north wing, their discoveries were grim. Flames had consumed everything in their path. In Room 212, 27 5th graders and the nun were dead, most asphyxiated by smoke. Next door, in Room 210, the nun and 29 4th graders had burned to death. At the end of the corridor, amid the debris from the partially collapsed roof, the badly-burned bodies of nine 7th graders were discovered huddled next to their nun near the front of Room 208. Across the hallway, in Rooms 209 and 211, another 27 8th graders lay dead.

For the hundreds of parents and relatives standing in stunned silence outside the school, the huge loss of life became apparent. As weary firefighters emerged from the ruined building carrying cloth-covered stretchers, a long line of ambulances and police squadrons crept slowly past to collect the bodies. For many parents the plight was made worse by not knowing if their children were alive or dead. Although many did locate their youngsters in the streets outside the school or in neighboring homes, others were left to search among the

Firefighters carry a body to an awaiting police squadron for the trip to the county morgue.

seven hospitals that had received the injured. For some parents, the search would not end until they reached the county morgue. By night's end, 90 bodies had been counted, 87 children and three nuns.

Chicago, a city tempered by past tragedies, was stunned by the appalling loss. In addition to the dead, another 100 people were injured, including students, school staff, firefighters, and civilians. Two families had each lost two children. Among the injured, some had fractured skulls, broken bones, smoke-damaged lungs, and terrible burns. Five more children died in the coming months, bringing the final death toll to 55 girls, 37 boys, and three nuns.

As the destroyed school still smoldered, questions arose: How did the fire start? How was it able to spread so fast? Why did it go unnoticed for up to 20 minutes? And why did so many perish?

Accusing fingers pointed in all directions. The church's pastor received death threats. Angry parents charged the fire department with slow response. Fire officials blamed school personnel for a delay in turning in an alarm. Candy store owner Barbara Glowacki was criticized for not letting Elmer Barkhaus use her telephone. The janitor was accused of poor housekeeping. The Archdiocese of Chicago was blamed for overcrowding. As newswires reported the disaster around the globe, the Pope sent personal condolences to the parish and its families, while the Soviet Union criticized the United States for spending too much money on weapons systems and less on safety devices for schools.

Investigators sifted the ruins to piece together the fire's rapid progression: sometime after 2 P.M., the blaze broke out in a ringed, 30-gallon cardboard trash drum located at the bottom of the school's northeast stairwell. After consuming refuse in the container, the fire at first simmered from a lack of oxygen

and smoldered undetected, elevating temperatures in the confined stairwell space. When intense heat shattered a window at the bottom of the stairwell, a fresh supply of oxygen was sucked into the area, causing the fire in the waste drum to

Fire-charred main corridor on the school's second floor. Note the collapsed roof.

flash up. The flames quickly spread to the unprotected wooden and asphalt-tile staircase, feeding off varnished woodwork and walls coated with 14 layers of paint, the top two layers composed of an extremely flammable rubberized-plastic paint that produced heavy black smoke.

The day after: unbelieving crowds flock to view the school.

Because the building had no sprinkler system, the stairwell quickly turned into a chimney as flames, smoke, and gases billowed up from the basement. A closed fire door on the first floor stopped the blaze from entering the first-floor corridor. But there was no door on the second floor, allowing the fire to continue up the stairway and sweep into the 85-foot-long corridor leading to the second-floor classrooms. Once inside the corridor the fire fed on combustible wooden flooring, walls, and trim, as well as the ceiling, which was also coated in the flammable rubberized-plastic paint, thus filling the corridor with deadly columns of penetrating black smoke. While the fire made its way up the stairwell, hot air and gases in the basement had entered a shaft in the basement wall and ascended two stories inside the wall. This hot air fanned out into the shallow cockloft above the second-floor ceiling, sparking serious secondary burning in the hidden area directly above the six north-wing classrooms packed with 323 students and six teachers. These flames also dropped into the second-floor corridor from two ventilator grilles in the ceiling.

Some survivors reported that after classroom doors had been opened and quickly closed, they heard a loud whoosh, thought to have come from an explosion that accompanied the ignition of volatile fire gases that had built up in the corridor. When intense heat from the fire began breaking large glass transoms over classroom doors, smoke and flames entered the rooms, spread across flammable ceiling tile, and forced the occupants to the windows. This was the situation in the school's north wing when the first firefighters arrived at 2:44 P.M. As they concentrated first on rescue, the fire on the upper story of the north wing grew steadily worse and eventually burned off one-third of the roof before being brought under control.

Though investigators were able to pinpoint the start of the fire, its cause eluded them. A check of the heating and electrical systems revealed no problems. And no evidence suggested the fire was fed by an accelerant. Several pupils were known to sneak cigarettes in the stairwell, but no solid evidence pointed to a discarded smoke as a possible cause. The only other possibility was arson.

The week after the fire, a blue-ribbon coroner's jury heard testimony from firefighters, church officials, students, teachers, and parents. The inquest revealed some disturbing facts: Our Lady of the Angels School, like many other school buildings at that time, had no sprinkler system or smoke detectors, and its fire alarm rang only in the building, it did not transmit a signal to the fire department. The nearest street fire alarm box was two blocks away. All but one of the school's staircases were open, without fire doors, and the building had just one fire escape. Window ledges were 37 inches from the floor—too high, it was learned, for some children to climb onto. Consequently, many of the dead had been found stacked beneath the windowsills. Finally, with an enrollment of approximately 1,400 students, the school was severely over-crowded.

Nevertheless, the school had passed its most recent fire inspection the previous October. Chicago's municipal code at the time did not apply to pre-ordinance buildings built before 1949. Instead, a 1905 law that lacked such modern safety requirements as sprinkler systems, automatic fire alarms, and enclosed stairways covered Our Lady of the Angels. It was later determined that a sprinkler system for the school would have cost about $8 per parent—the same price as one football helmet used by the school's 8th-grade football team.

Despite all its hoopla, the coroner's jury failed to find the fire's cause and did little more than issue 22 non-binding recommendations for providing schools in the city with more extensive fire protection. Among them were calls for sprinkler systems, fire detection systems, alarm boxes outside every school, and fire-safe construction. Public outrage, however, resulted in sweeping changes in school fire codes throughout the country. In Chicago, the city council passed legislation designed to prevent the tragedy from ever being repeated. Schools two or more stories in height were required to be sprinklered, and all new schools had to have enclosed stairways and be built of fire-resistant construction. Laws also required that fire alarm boxes be located no more than 100 feet from a school's front door, and school fire alarms had to be connected directly to the fire department.

Many parents were angered by the inquest proceedings, claiming they did more to shield the Archdiocese of Chicago from embarrassment and liability than to provide pertinent information relating to their children's deaths. Left substantially unanswered were two big questions: the delay in sounding the fire alarm in the school and the fire's cause. Most officials agreed the rule permitting only the mother superior to ring the alarm influenced the early confusion. Fire Commissioner Robert Quinn blamed the high number of deaths on this delay in notifying the fire department, noting that once they were finally called, it took firefighters only two minutes to reach the scene. Another circumstance cited by Quinn was the wrong address Mrs. Maloney gave the fire alarm office; she told firefighters to go to 3808 W. Iowa St., the address of the church. In fact, the burning school was half a block around the corner, at 909 N. Avers Ave. Quinn also refuted claims that fire department ladders were too short to reach the victims. Several painting ladders had been put up by neighbors and church personnel before the fire department's arrival, however all but one was too short. The exception was a ladder placed by the school's assistant janitor that enabled an estimated 25 children to reach safety.

No grand jury was ever convened to hear evidence of possible criminal negligence, despite a scathing report issued in 1959 by the National Fire Protection Association that placed blame on city and archdiocesan officials "who have failed to recognize their life-safety obligations in housing children in structures which are firetraps."[4] But in 1965, a panel of three Cook County judges did order the Chicago archdiocese to pay a total of $3.2 million to 76 injured victims and 90 families whose children died in the fire. Five families filed lawsuits against the church, but in the end every family who lost a child was given $7,500, regardless of whether a suit was filed. Families of injured pupils received smaller cash settlements. About $1 million in additional funds to cover funerals and medical expenses was paid by Catholic Charities and a special fund set up by Mayor Richard J. Daley.

AFTER FADING from public consciousness, in January 1962, the school fire once again became front-page news when police in suburban Cicero, Illinois, questioned a 13-year-old boy about a series of fires he had set in the western suburb. When the police learned that the boy had been a troubled 5th grader at Our Lady of the Angels at the time of the fire, they pressed him for more information. His mother and stepfather hired an attorney, who recommended that the boy submit to a lie detector test.

In his interview with the boy, Chicago polygraph expert John Reid learned that the youth's firesetting tendencies stretched back to the age of five, when he first set fire to a garage. Reid learned the youth had set up to 11 fires in apartment buildings in Chicago and Cicero, mostly by tossing matches onto papers placed at the bottom of stairways. At first,

Memorial to the school fire dead at Queen of Heaven Cemetery in suburban Hillside, Illinois.

nuns sitting in heaven who want the truth."[5]

The boy, Reid testified, then "became evasive, turning his eyes from side to side, and then told me how he started the Our Lady of the Angels fire." The boy admitted to Reid that he started the fire in the hopes that any damage would be just enough to allow for a couple of extra days off from school. The boy also told Reid he had set the fire because he hated his teachers and his principal, who, he said, "always wanted to expel me from school." The boy's attendance record at the school was poor, and his behavior was listed as "deplorable." His teachers, a report shows, said he was a "troublemaker."[6]

In his eight-page confession, the boy described how he started the fire in the basement after going to the washroom. "I looked around and I didn't see anybody. I threw three matches in the can and then I ran up the stairs to my room." The boy also filled in a pencil sketch of the basement, pinpointing exactly where the fire was started. He said he waited at the trash barrel for "a few minutes" after setting the fire and watched the flames "get bigger and bigger." He then returned to his room on the second floor and was evacuated with his class.[7]

When Reid asked why he had never before told anyone about setting fire to the school, the boy replied, "I was afraid my dad was going to give me a beating and I'd get in trouble with the police and I'd get the electric chair or something." Reid turned the confession over to authorities, and the boy was placed in the Audy Juvenile Home. Chicago police pursued a juvenile petition charging him in the school fire, but after a series of closed-door Family Court hearings that ended in March 1962, Judge Alfred Cilella threw out the boy's confession, ruling that Reid had obtained it improperly. Moreover, because the boy was under 13 at the time of the fire, the judge said he could not be tried for a felony in Illinois. Nevertheless, the judge found the youth delinquent for starting

the boy denied that he had set the Our Lady of the Angels fire, but the test results suggested he was lying. In a Family Court hearing in February 1962, Reid described how he leaned over to the boy and said to him, "There are 92 children and three the Cicero fires, and he sent him away to a home for troubled boys in Michigan.

Despite the judge's ruling, the boy's description of how, where, and when the fire was started, details that only the fire setter would have known, corroborated much information compiled by investigators that, up to 1962, had been previously unreleased. Also telling are the similarities in the way the fires started in the apartment buildings and school, blazes that began in papers in a stairwell, further supporting the claims of Reid and other investigators who remained convinced that the boy was being truthful in his confession.

IN FEBRUARY 1959, the remains of the school building were razed to make way for a new one—a $1 million edifice made of concrete, glass, and steel. The new school opened in 1960 and remained in operation until 1999, when it was closed due to low enrollment in a community whose demographics had changed dramatically. After the school closed, survivors placed a plaque in its front lobby to commemorate the 1958 fire. Another memorial, an impressive granite shrine erected in 1960 by the parish's then pastor, Monsignor Joseph Cussen, sits inside Queen of Heaven cemetery in suburban Hillside, Illinois, where 25 fire victims lie buried together. But perhaps the most fitting monument to the dead was the new school itself, which, when it opened, was equipped with a full complement of fire safety devices, including a red fire-alarm box just inside its front doors.

Aside from the occasional anniversary story, the Our Lady of the Angels fire passed into history, assuming its position as America's third-worst school catastrophe and Chicago's third-deadliest fire. And like all great disasters, it left its own legacy in the form of vastly improved school fire safety laws, though at a cost of 95 lives.

Aerial view of the original McCormick Place.

Fire and Ice: McCormick Place

McCormick Place was Chicago's showpiece $35-million, 10-acre lakefront exposition and convention hall when on January 16, 1967, one of the costliest fires in U.S. history destroyed the enormous structure. A building labeled "incombustible" by its designers, in reality it proved as vulnerable to fire as Mrs. O'Leary's barn.

Situated next to Lake Michigan at 23rd Street, McCormick Place was the largest, most prestigious convention center in the United States, and its 1960 opening had crowned Chicago the convention capital of the nation. By being able to house major trade shows, local civic and business leaders had hoped McCormick Place would make Chicago an international center for commerce and trade. It did. The shows it hosted drew big crowds, enabling the local economy to reap millions of dollars in annual profits from conventioneers who patronized the city's many central hotels, restaurants, and nightclubs.

For Richard J. Daley, Chicago's paternal and patriarchal mayor, McCormick Place was one more notch in his list of legacy-building accomplishments. Since taking office in 1955, the mayor had overseen construction of a new airport, new expressways, and a new urban campus for the University of Illinois at Chicago. To make way for the university, the city first had to clear a large tract of land. It accomplished this by bulldozing one of Chicago's greatest ethnic enclaves, the Taylor Street "Little Italy" neighborhood. Forced to relocate their homes and businesses, many Italian-Americans who had supported Daley felt betrayed and never forgave him. By the 1990s, the university's geopolitical tentacles stretched even further, causing the demise of the fabled Maxwell Street Market, erasing from view another link to Chicago's storied past.

But of all the infrastructure improvements launched during his reign, McCormick Place stood among the mayor's personal crowning achievements. The facility was named after Colonel Robert R. McCormick, the late archconservative publisher of the *Chicago Tribune*, who during a privileged lifetime that ended in 1955, had purchased his own commission in the U.S. Army and then later, as a newspaper baron, tried to simplify the English language. McCormick had been among those who supported the controversial idea of building a large lakefront convention center for Chicago, and he used the *Tribune*'s political clout to get legislation passed forming a public convention center authority that would create and fund the undertaking. Though architect Daniel Burnham's 1909 grand plan for Chicago prescribed an unbroken string of lakefront parks whose shoreline should remain "forever open, clear and free," it was only through a delicate balance of wisdom, strength, and political cunning that Mayor Daley and his supporters were able to sidestep Burnham's ideal and secure the $40 million in public funding needed to finance construction of the huge project, a venture others before him had tried and failed.[1] The quest finally came to fruition in 1958, when ground was broken along the lakefront at 23rd Street on the site of the 1933 Century of Progress World's Fair at Burnham Park. Two years later, in November 1960, the convention hall opened by hosting the National Home and Flower Show.

The enormity of the McCormick Place building matched the ego of its namesake. Designed by Alfred Shaw and made primarily of concrete and steel, the mammoth windowless structure spanned an area three city blocks long by one city block wide and stood the equivalent of seven stories high. At its south end was the 5,000-seat Arie Crown Theater, that would become renowned for its excellent acoustics. The convention center itself had three principal floors, with the main or upper level consisting of a 320,000-square-foot exhibit hall, the interior of which was as long as six football fields. Banquet halls and meeting rooms occupied the middle level, while the first level was actually in the basement and contained an additional 180,000 square feet of exhibit space. The structural system on the upper level made use of 18 massive steel trusses to hold up the roof; this truss system not only provided support but also permitted unobstructed floor space to accommodate the large trade shows booked regularly into McCormick Place. The two lower floors were built of reinforced concrete. The ceiling in the main hall reached 40 feet high while the basement ceiling was 12 feet high.

Even though insurance underwriters considered McCormick Place virtually fireproof, every effort was made to protect the facility against the remotest threat of fire. Fourteen city fire alarm boxes were strategically placed throughout the building, as was every type of fire extinguisher, and four additional city fire alarm boxes were located on its outside. In addition, a 1,500-gallon-per-minute pump supplied water to 69 standpipe hose stations and an automatic sprinkler system was fitted with 1,122 sprinklers. This fire protection system was serviced by its own unattended pumping station located a quarter-mile away from the main building. Its four pumps could deliver 10,000 gallons of water per minute from a 24-inch branch running off a 36-inch city water main. The pumping station also fed the seven fire hydrants placed around McCormick Place's perimeter. Three other hydrants in the area were supplied by a Chicago Park District water main.

Chicagoans have an unabashed pride in their city and its many landmarks, from cultural gems like the University of Chicago and a slew of world-class museums to the city's famous architecture and tree-lined system of boulevard-connected parks. McCormick Place became one more high-profile asset, one poised to serve its city for many years to come.

Or so it was thought.

On Sunday evening, January 15, 1967, workmen were preparing the final arrangements for the 46th semiannual tradeshow of the National Housewares Manufacturers Association, scheduled to open the following morning. An estimated 30,000 people were expected to attend the weeklong event marketing the latest in kitchen and household technology. The huge show included 1,234 exhibits occupying 3,700 booths. Of these exhibits, 608 were set up on the main upper-level exhibition floor; the remaining 626 occupied space in the basement hall. Booths on the upper level measured ten feet wide by 15 feet long, and the smaller cubicles in the basement were ten feet by ten feet. A number of larger displays

The fireboat *Joseph Medill* was assigned to the McCormick Place fire. The boat was named after the *Chicago Tribune* founder and former Chicago mayor who had been elected on the "Fireproof Ticket" in 1871, following the Great Chicago Fire.

on the upper level took up several booth spaces, some exceeding 15 feet in height and incorporating narrow wood-strip canopied ceilings. All exhibits were built with a variety of combustible materials, mainly plywood and wood pegboard, and each was decorated with curtains, bunting, and canopy fabrics. The exhibits displayed a wide array of housewares, gadgets, and dry goods. Products included various paper goods; flammable liquids; pressurized cans of hair spray, lacquers, cleaning solutions; and other items made of rubber, plastic, cardboard, and cotton. Added to this were stacks of cardboard boxes, crates, and other combustible storage containers. When factored together, the fuel load inside McCormick Place that night exceeded 4,000 tons, equal to an entire city block of dry woodsheds. The convention hall had been turned into a vast open exhibit area that had nothing in place to stop the spread of a fire: no firewalls, fire-resistive partitions, or other protective barriers.

At midnight Monday, January 16, about 150 people continued to work inside the building, including janitors, maintenance personnel, and numerous private security guards. Their work was devoted largely to last-minute details such as installing carpet between display floor aisles and inside exhibit booths. At 2:05 A.M., two janitors sweeping up in Aisle 100 on the upper level noticed smoke rising from behind a large display behind Booths 178, 180, and 182. This site was next to the building's west wall in approximately the center of the structure and immediately north of a set of exit doors. Upon finding a small fire burning near the carpeted floor, the janitors tried beating it out with their brooms, dumping several pails of water on it, and emptying four fire extinguishers. Their efforts failed and the fire quickly spread up the booth's fiberboard walls, igniting numerous packaged articles. A security supervisor radioed his control desk, ordering that the fire

The *Joseph Medill* fireboat fights another fire along the Chicago River.

department be called. A standpipe fire hose station and a fire alarm box linked directly to the fire department was located less than 100 feet from the fire; however, neither was utilized.

At 2:11 A.M., a telephone call reporting the fire was logged at the main fire alarm office in City Hall. Because McCormick Place was a major target hazard that called for a full, first alarm assignment, operators began tapping out Box 798, a response consisting of four engine companies, two hook-and-ladders, two squad companies, one snorkel, one fog pressure, one salvage truck, and a battalion chief. Engine 37, the fireboat *Joseph Medill*, also was assigned. (The fireboat was named after the former Chicago mayor who had been elected on the "Fireproof Ticket" in 1871, following the Great Chicago Fire. Ironically, Medill, who founded the *Chicago Tribune* in 1847, was the grandfather of Robert R. McCormick, whose name adorned the ill-fated building to which firefighters were now responding.)

The temperature in downtown Chicago that morning was a biting 13 degrees, but it was even colder along the lakefront thanks to a raw 25-m.p.h. wind that whipped off the water. First-due Engine 8 and Truck 4 pulled out of their Chinatown firehouse and sped to the scene, as did Chief Ted Latas of the 9th Battalion, also based there. When they arrived at McCormick Place, fire was visible from the west side through the center glass exit doors north of the main entrance. Also seen was a glowing metal freight door 25 feet north of the exit.

Latas ordered Engine 8 and Truck 4 to stretch three large hoselines into the main exhibition hall and connect to the nearest fire hydrant and to force open the freight doors. The next three engine companies were ordered to stretch two hoselines each and hook up to the remaining six hydrants along the front of the building. Firefighters from Trucks 4 and 14 hurried to the roof to cut open a hole for ventilation. All

were routine tasks for the highly capable firefighters. But when Latas stepped inside the exhibition hall to further plot his strategy, what he encountered was anything but a routine fire. An enormous inferno was raging with enough fuel and oxygen to cause the loss of the entire building. By now the fire had overtaken a large area in the main level and was heading east and west. Latas had his aide call for a second alarm. "It's really rolling," he told the alarm office.[2]

Latas next ordered the crew from the high-pressure wagon to use their two small attack lines in a futile attempt to cut off the fire from the clear areas. Engine companies followed with heavier lines, but in minutes, the fire had almost completely surrounded the hose teams. To make matters worse, the fire hydrants outside the building didn't work, leaving the fireground without a water supply. The failure was later traced to inoperative underground gate valves in the grid system supplying the fire hydrants. The hydrants, authorities later learned, had not been properly maintained by the Metropolitan Fair and Exposition Authority, operator of the convention center. Another closed gate valve also prevented water from being drawn by the park district main. Of the seven hydrants surrounding the building, only the two at the northwest corner worked. Moreover, inside the much-acclaimed pumphouse, two of the four pumps supplying the sprinkler and standpipe systems also malfunctioned, leaving the sprinkler system useless. Instead of supplying the rated 10,000 gallons-per-minute to the system, only about a quarter of the capacity was available and with very low pressure. Only five sprinkler heads eventually opened. This was no match for the flames, and it spelled doom for McCormick Place.

With fire surrounding them, the firefighters were ordered to drop their hoses and retreat. A third alarm was transmitted and another attempt was made to re-enter the building and attack

Crews pour water onto the ruins of McCormick Place. Note the massive steel truss system that failed to support the building's roof.

the fire with the standpipe system. This too proved useless thanks to the low water pressure. A huge firestorm was now whipping inside McCormick Place, fanned by a fierce wind that blew through the doors held open by firehoses. With no interior walls in place, flames spread throughout the entire upper exhibition area, then shifted direction and headed south toward the Arie Crown Theater. That's when all firefighters were ordered out of the building and off the roof. The time had come to mount an exterior attack, a "surround and drown." Firefighters knew they couldn't save the main building, but maybe they could stop the fire from overtaking the theater.

Before long the 18 steel trusses supporting the roof began to sway and bend from the intense heat. Within 45 minutes of the first alarm they failed, causing the roof to collapse and sending tons of debris and the large ventilating system down into the structure. Large portions of the exterior masonry panel walls also caved in. Now with an endless supply of fresh air from the open roof, flames shot 100 feet into the air and completely devoured all of the remaining fuel inside the main exhibition hall. The fire had also spread into the basement, sparking a large secondary blaze.

At 2:53 A.M., the fireboat *Medill* tied up to the east side of the building, its turret guns shooting large caliber streams onto the upper exhibition floor, which by then was completely engulfed by flames. The fire was elevated to five alarms plus five special calls, bringing an armada of 97 pieces of equipment and 500 firefighters. Two other fireboats, the *Victor L. Schlaeger* and the *Fred Busse*, also responded from berths up to 90 minutes away. The *Busse* took a position along the south end of the building and, using its powerful master streams as a giant water curtain, cut the fire off before it spread into the Arie Crown Theater. The theater was spared thanks to two other factors: the presence of a large brick firewall that had

been built between it and the exhibition hall, and the fact that the fire simply began to run out of fuel. When the *Schlaeger* arrived at 4 A.M., it docked at the north end of the building.

Meanwhile, to secure an adequate water supply for the fire companies parked around the building, firefighters set up a massive relay operation and began pumping water to the fireground from city-supplied fire hydrants several hundred feet south and east of it. Each of the fireboats also drafted water from Lake Michigan to supply the land companies positioned around the building. The relay operation was reportedly the longest in the fire department's history; eventually enough hose was used to wrap around McCormick Place 14 times. As the three fireboats pounded away at the flames, the spray from their turret nozzles formed an icy slope on the east side of the building next to the lake, and together with the vibrations from the pumpers, caused equipment including a snorkel to slip dangerously close to the water's edge. Consequently, only four engines were used to draft water here, two of which had to be tied by ropes to nearby trees to prevent them from sliding into the lake. Eventually the flames began to darken as various fire apparatus, along with the three fireboats, moved alongside the crumbled walls to pour thousands of gallons of water onto the collapsed remains of the structure. Because there were no windows, the fire could not be completely extinguished from the outside until it had burned through the roof. Finally, after spending almost ten hours in the bitter cold, firefighters brought the fire under control. At 9:46 A.M., Fire Commissioner Robert J. Quinn declared the fire "struck out."

That morning Chicagoans couldn't believe McCormick Place lay in a twisted heap of smoldering ruins. Leading the shocked pack was Mayor Daley himself. After touring the site, Daley's directive was simple: "Find out what happened."

Results of the investigation by the Mayor's Committee to

Investigate the McCormick Place Fire were released July 1967. The fire originated in the rear center of the three-booth space where the janitors had first spotted smoke in the upper main floor hall. Though the exact cause of the fire could not be determined because of the extent of damage, remains of electrical wiring found behind the booth of origin pointed to substandard electrical connections as the likely source. Despite repeated attempts, investigators were never allowed by contractors to interview the electricians who had wired the booths in question. Moreover, the report pointed to a six-minute delay in calling the fire department after workers first tried to put out the fire. If workers had been properly trained in basic fire procedures, investigators noted, they would have known to first pull the interior fire alarm box and then utilize the standpipe hose located less than 100 feet from the source of the fire.

Poor maintenance of the fire hydrant system and the fire pump house and the fact that some underground hydrant valves in the grid were shut off and never turned back on after construction of the nearby Stevenson Expressway also contributed to the huge loss. Also revealed was the inadequacy of the building's sprinkler system. Despite the presence of over 1,100 sprinkler heads, the report said, only eight percent of the entire structure was in fact sprinklered, and no sprinklers were located in the main exhibition hall. Why? Because the steel roof trusses inside the hall were fireproofed up to a height of 20 feet above the floor, a distance thought to be more than adequate. What designers had failed to anticipate was the large amount of fuel inside the hall and the consequent effect of heat released in a rapidly burning fire. The heat and flames easily extended beyond this 20-foot level, impinging on the trusses holding up the 40-foot high ceiling, causing them to fail within minutes. Moreover, the fire in the basement level was sparked

Another view of the fire-ruined McCormick Place.

not by any direct flame contact from the main fire but from hot melted aluminum that had flowed downward through two open expansion joints running between support columns in the upper and lower level floors. The flow had originated from coverings on aluminum partition panels stored at four locations on the upper level. Utilizing handlines supplied by fireboats, firefighters were able to limit damage in this area to approximately 60 percent of the booths. Remaining booths received smoke, heat, and water damage.

Miraculously there was only one fatality. Twelve hours after the fire was reported, firefighters found the badly burned body of a 30-year-old security guard in the north end of the upper level. Fire officials believe he became disoriented and trapped by the rapidly moving flames and, in a desperate attempt to save himself, pulled an interior fire alarm. It is mind-boggling to consider what may have resulted if the fire had occurred eight hours later, when the building would have been filled with thousands of people attending the housewares show.

With a total loss of $52 million, the McCormick Place fire represented what was up to that time the costliest single building fire in the United States. As the investigation showed, this fire was lost not on the *fireground* but on the *drawing board*. Firefighters summoned to the scene took an enormous physical beating. Once again they proved themselves capable as ever, particularly considering the efficiency with which they performed the complicated relay pumping, an operation requiring great coordination.

In the end, McCormick Place became another Chicago phoenix to rise from the ashes, thanks largely in part to Daley, who the morning after the fire, vowed to rebuild the convention center. Using proceeds from insurance settlements as well as numerous public sources, a newer, bigger, more spectacular McCormick Place was erected on the same site and opened in 1970. Sleek and dramatic, the modern black steel building featured a more linear design than its predecessor. Two decades later, under a new mayor, Richard M. Daley, the facility was expanded further. A second hall was added in 1986, and a third in 1996, providing a total of 2.2-million square feet of exhibition space, making it the largest convention center in the country and Chicago the unquestioned capital of the convention industry. About 4 million people visit McCormick Place annually, pouring over $5 billion into the local economy. A state-of-the-art fire protection system guards the entire facility. The Arie Crown Theater is all that remains of the original structure.

Like the Iroquois Theater fire 63 years earlier, the case of the first McCormick Place serves as another reminder that, given the right conditions, even so-called "fireproof" buildings will burn.

(*Left*) Nighttime along Madison Street during the riots of April 4, 5, and 6, 1968. Fires broke out all across the west side following the death of Martin Luther King, Jr. Many neighborhoods never recovered. (*Right*) Severely outnumbered by rioters, police were powerless to prevent looting of the mostly white-owned shops.

A Burning Fury

The 1960s became a point of demarcation for the United States, one that brought great and irreversible change to the country's social fabric. All across the nation, young people were seeking self-expression, rebelling against the norms of their parents, and denouncing government policies, including America's growing involvement in the unpopular war in Vietnam. The decade also saw expansion of the civil rights movement, its momentum driven largely by the efforts of Dr. Martin Luther King, Jr. While younger and more militant black leaders advocated armed confrontation as a means to achieve justice and equality, Dr. King remained undaunted as a voice for social change through peaceful protest. Most African-Americans saw him as a symbol of hope. In 1965, he received the Nobel Peace Prize in recognition of his efforts.

The following year, Dr. King brought his protest movement to Chicago, his first foray into the North, where he hoped to address various problems faced by urban blacks, mainly in housing and employment discrimination. Even though Chicago had a sizable population of African-Americans, housing had been problematic for them since the 1880s, when they first began to arrive in the city in numbers. First settling in an area on the south side dubbed the Black Belt, by 1900, Chicago's African-American inhabitants had grown to 40,000. Lured by the promise of industrial jobs, this number doubled during 1916-18 when laborers were needed to meet increases in manufacturing brought about by war production. Much of this great migration to the industrial North from the rural, agrarian South was prompted by stories in the *Defender*, Chicago's black newspaper, which encouraged southern blacks to relocate north. But the city's majority and sometimes openly antagonistic white populace did not always welcome blacks who came to Chicago. As a result, the housing stock available to African-Americans stayed fairly limited and failed to keep pace with the growing needs brought on by ever-increasing arrivals. Consequently, the Black Belt remained geographically restrictive and densely populated, containing some of the worst slums in the city. In time a heightening sense of unrest began festering inside the crowded black ghetto, and by the end of World War I, racial tensions in Chicago were reaching dangerously volatile levels. Starting around 1917, when African-Americans began moving further south into the Washington Park area, whites responded violently, bombing 23 black homes. Racial unease continued to build until the summer of 1919, when it could no longer be contained. On July 27, a black teenager named Eugene Williams crossed an invisible line of segregation when, while swimming in Lake Michigan, he accidentally drifted into the waters off the "white only" 29th Street beach. When people on shore noticed that the youth was in their zone, they began throwing rocks at him. One report says Williams was hit in the head, lost consciousness, and went under. The official coroner's report says he was too scared to come ashore and, after clinging to a piece of wood for a lengthy period, drowned after becoming too fatigued to stay afloat. Regardless of which version is true, Williams's death touched off some of the worst racial violence Chicago has ever seen. During the ensuing five days of rioting, many homes were set ablaze as angry mobs of both races roamed the streets of the city's south side, savagely beating each other and spreading a wave of costly vandalism. It took the combined effort of the Illinois National Guard and a fierce rainstorm to quell the uproar that resulted in the deaths of 38 people: 23 of them black, 15 white. Another 300 people were injured. Despite its toll, the 1919 riot would not be Chicago's last case of racially-motivated civil unrest. The conditions that sparked it would worsen considerably, making the event a mere precursor of things to come.

When the second great black migration ended after World War II, a half million African-Americans called Chicago home. By the late 1950s, this number had again nearly doubled. Black Chicagoans began moving from their traditional south side enclave to the rapidly-changing west side, in neighborhoods set along Madison Street as well as in Lawndale, Garfield Park, and Austin on Chicago's far western edge. As whites moved out and blacks moved in, many neighborhoods quickly fell into disrepair and became desperately poor, creating hostility among residents who were becoming increasingly agitated over the lack of economic opportunities in their communities. By the mid-1960s, Chicago's changing industrial and population base also gave rise to a growing surplus of aging and in many cases unsafe empty buildings. The situation mirrored that of other northern industrial cities, where once-thriving neighborhoods declined as businesses and white residents relocated to the rapidly-developing suburbs, leaving behind vacant factories and warehouses that in time became the target of vagrants, vandals, and arsonists.

By the time Dr. King arrived in Chicago in 1966, racial tensions in the city had once again reached new highs. An ugly example of this unease was seen that August, when during an open-housing march through Marquette Park, Dr. King was hit in the head with a stone as his group made its way past thousands of jeering and taunting whites who shouted racial epithets and tossed rocks. The incident made news and caused King to label Chicago the "Selma of the North." Still, he remained determined in his cause, renting an apartment in Lawndale, where he stayed for eight months until securing an agreement with Chicago's real estate board, whose members had pledged to abide by the city's open housing ordinance that forbade discriminatory selling practices. But handshakes to the contrary, little changed in Chicago following King's departure. Such failures and repeated double-crosses had caused America's black ghettos to smolder all the more, the distrust of whites fueled by increasing frustration over the gap between promise and performance in civil rights. Many black youths, discouraged by the slow pace of change, began venting their anger through open, explosive disobedience. Between 1964 and 1967, 58 American cities erupted in riots that left 225 people dead and nearly 5,000 injured. These riots began spontaneously after minor incidents between police and African-Americans blew up into urban warfare, resulting in terrible losses of life and property. In August 1965, the black Watts section of Los Angeles exploded in burning and looting after a police officer pulled over a black motorist. Before it ended, more than 100 fires had been set, leaving a 150-block section of Los Angeles in ruins. In July 1967, a similar situation occurred in Newark after police arrested a black cab driver. Stores were looted and bombed and the National Guard was called out. During the four days of turbulence, a 38-year-old white fire captain was killed by a sniper while fighting an arson fire in the riot zone. That same month in Detroit, a routine raid on an illegal all-night tavern in the heart of the black ghetto drew a crowd that quickly became angry and out of control. The result was the worst race riot of the decade. When the five days of arson and looting ended, 42 people were dead and nearly 400 were injured. During that long hot summer of 1967, $44 million worth of property crumbled in Detroit. It was an event from which the Motor City never recovered; most business and property owners never rebuilt and many families moved away.

Chicago had not escaped the violence. One day after the Watts riot broke out, on August 13, 1965, trouble erupted in Garfield Park when a fire department ladder truck manned by a crew of white firefighters lost control while pulling out of its firehouse at Pulaski Road and Wilcox Street, striking and killing a black female pedestrian. The result saw four nights of rioting by angry blacks, many of whom had been complaining for some time about the racial makeup of that particular fire station headquartered in what had by then become a predominantly African-American neighborhood. The following June, Puerto Ricans in Humboldt Park rioted after a police officer shot and killed a 21-year-old man. Burning, looting, and brick throwing continued for two days along Division Street before peace was finally restored. Though the rioting in these

two instances had been limited to the immediate neighborhoods in which it erupted, authorities dismissed their symptoms as isolated incidents triggered by lawless instigators. But the next time widespread rioting visited Chicago, the mark it left would be indelible, its cause undeniable.

ON WEDNESDAY, April 3, 1968, Dr. Martin Luther King, Jr. went to Memphis to march in support of striking city sanitation workers, the majority of whom were black. That evening, Dr. King made his famous mountaintop speech in which he foretold his future by conceding that he "might not make it" with them to the "Promised Land."

"I don't know what will happen now," Dr. King prophesied. "We've got some difficult days ahead."

The following morning saw King step from his room at the Lorraine Motel onto a second-floor balcony. Seconds later a shot rang out and the 39-year-old civil rights leader fell dead in a pool of blood. Indignation over Dr. King's assassination drew a quick and angry response from many in the black community who turned from his message of peaceful demonstration to wage war. Violence broke out in 41 U.S. cities, where mobs of irate African-Americans took to the streets throwing rocks, shooting guns, looting stores, and burning buildings.

In Chicago, news of the assassination spread quickly, and great distress was felt in the black neighborhoods on the city's west side. That Friday, angry black high school students marched out of their classrooms. Soon after, the west side of Chicago exploded in an orgy of uncontrolled looting and burning. The rioters chose west Madison Street as their battle-ground, an avenue comprised mainly of storefronts and apartments buildings that ran straight through the black ghetto. Angry mobs descended upon the street like an

Litter covers the street as firefighters work to contain one of the 125 major fires that erupted during the three days of rioting.

Fire commissioner Robert J. Quinn, who commanded the Chicago Fire Department from 1955 to 1978. During the 1968 riots, he directed the battle against the fires by helicopter.

invading army, smashing store windows and plundering shelves. White shopkeepers escaped with their lives, some beaten and kicked as they fled their businesses. Automobiles with white drivers were pelted with bottles and bricks, their occupants pulled from the vehicles and beaten. "A white man killed Martin Luther King," the rioters chanted.[1] The rampage was on.

As word of the rioting spread, downtown Chicago emptied quickly. Nervousness gave way to panic as people left work early. After imploring for calm and releasing a statement that read, "Violence in a free society leads to anarchy, and anarchy accomplishes nothing," Mayor Daley issued his now infamous directive ordering police to "shoot to kill" any arsonist, and to "shoot to maim" any looter.[2] By Friday evening, the first of 6,000 National Guard troops were pressed into action to assist Chicago police. When it became apparent that more help was needed, acting Illinois Governor Samuel Shapiro called on President Lyndon B. Johnson to send in federal troops.

For the Chicago Fire Department, the west side riots marked one of the busiest periods in its history. About 2,000 firefighters utilizing more than 100 pieces of equipment were required to control the biggest conflagration the city had seen since the 1934 stockyards fire. Just two days before King's assassination, the fire department had extinguished a huge blaze that swept the enormous Ford City warehouse, reputed at the time to be the world's largest single-story structure. But as exhausting as the Ford City fire was for Chicago's firefighters, they were about to be taken to an even greater task.

It began at 3:49 Friday afternoon, when a fire touched off by arsonists broke out inside a large furniture warehouse in the 2300 block of west Madison Street. The blaze was quickly elevated to a 5-11 alarm, bringing an armada of fire equipment to the scene. Other fires were started almost simultaneously along a two-mile stretch of Madison Street from approximately

National Guard troops protect fire apparatus, including a fuel truck.
Gasoline trucks made easy targets for rioters bent on thwarting firefighters' efforts.

Leavitt Street (2200 west) to about Kostner Avenue (4400 west). Widespread burning also erupted in the vicinity of 16th Street and Lawndale Avenue, Roosevelt Road between California Avenue and Independence Boulevard, and Fifth Avenue between Jackson Boulevard and Central Avenue. For the most part, vandals were indiscriminate in their choice of targets: they set fire to small mom-and-pop businesses as well as the big-name department stores in the busy Madison-Pulaski shopping district.

Because they were so greatly outnumbered, all the police could do was stand aside and watch. After lighting fires with gasoline or other incendiary means, rioters would wait for firefighters to arrive, then hurl bricks and bottles at them and, in some cases, begin shooting. Firefighters were ordered to stay clear of areas where gunfire was reported; however, before the violence had ended, one firefighter was shot in the ankle, a police officer in the arm.

As sunset arrived that Friday, plumes of black smoke blanketed large sections of the west side. In some locations, heavy smoke cut visibility to half a block. As radio and television stations broadcast messages calling for all off-duty firefighters to report to work, suburban fire departments sent equipment to cover empty Chicago fire stations. By 10 P.M. that night, the firefighters' job had become hopeless. As the firestorms burned both sides of Madison Street, telephone calls reporting them to the main fire alarm office in city hall came in faster than they could be fielded. As many as 36 major blazes were burning out of control, some without any fire companies sent to fight them, others with only one or two units assigned. All the while, vandals opened fire hydrants, causing water pressure to drop. Because regular fuel trucks made too easy a target for rioters, gasoline was smuggled to fire trucks in unmarked vehicles. As the night wore on, fire companies moved from one blaze to the next. "Just pick a fire and go to work," alarm operators directed them.[3]

Eventually the fire situation on the west side became so bad that commanders in the field changed their strategy from offense to defense, opting to let the large, uncontrolled fires burn freely while attempting to block flames from spreading to adjoining structures. Police did what they could to protect the firefighters, who endured rocks and bottles and threats of violence. "We're gonna burn down this whole town and you with it," shouted one knife-wielding man as he ran past a group of firefighters.[4] Still, the firefighters pressed on, pouring thousands of gallons of water on scores of burning buildings, even though at times it seemed futile.

On Saturday, major rioting had spread to two other black neighborhoods, Woodlawn on the south side and Division and Sedgwick Streets on the north side, the latter of which saw police, firefighters, and National Guardsmen pinned down by sniper fire coming from a high-rise in the Cabrini-Green housing project. When police and National Guard troops stormed the 12th floor of the building at 1230 N. Larrabee St., they found the 18-year-old gunman dead from a bullet wound to the head. It was never learned who fired the fatal shot. Not far from the shooting, in Old Town, windows were smashed along a stretch of North Avenue between Wells and Halsted Streets; while in the Loop, black youths smashed more windows after leaving a staged demonstration in front of City Hall. A 7 o'clock curfew had been set Saturday evening for people under 21 years old, and an emergency order issued by Mayor Daley banned the sale of liquor, ammunition, guns, and gasoline in portable containers. Though the violence had diminished somewhat, it was far from over. Structures still burned and firefighters continued to be shot at. The next morning, Palm Sunday, saw the arrival of regular Army troops outfitted with M-16s and hand grenades. It was the first time federal troops had been needed to put down racial violence in Chicago.

By the time order was restored the next day, the riot area on the west side resembled a war zone. "I never thought that this would happen here," Mayor Daley said after touring the affected areas in a helicopter.[5] The damage was indeed appalling. Broken bricks and shards of glass littered the landscape along a 28-block stretch of Madison Street, where many buildings had been reduced in spots to smoldering heaps of rubble. In some areas, whole blocks had been burned to the ground. The worst of the arson occurred on Madison Street between Kedzie and Homan Avenues, where nearly every building had been destroyed. Bulldozers were brought in to clear the wreckage and knock down unsafe structures.

Restoring order to Chicago required the combined resources of 11,000 police, 6,000 National Guardsmen, and 5,000 federal army troops as well as the 2,000 firefighters. During the nearly four days of rioting, between ten and 12 civilians—all of them African-American males between the ages of 16 and 34—had died from knife wounds, gunshots, or burns. Another 500 people were injured. There were 300 arrests and 250 major cases of looting reported. One hundred twenty-five major fires destroyed 170 buildings, leaving 1,000 people homeless. The final damage estimate from the rioting exceeded $10 million.[6] That the riots were an expression of deep emotion and frustration as well as a spontaneous response to a common grief felt in the wake of Dr. King's killing was obvious. Black leaders laid responsibility at the feet of the nation's white power structure, blaming it for the conditions that precipitated the rebellion.

Following the waves of urban violence that broke out in 1967, the National Advisory Commission on Civil Disorders (the Kerner Commission), chaired by then Illinois Gov. Otto Kerner, found that the United States had become "two Americas—one white, one black, separate but unequal."[7] The findings were equally relevant to what had occurred in Chicago and other cities following King's killing; the report became an indictment against white America, which it said had allowed 300 years of racism to be bred into the very fabric of American society. "Segregation and poverty have created in the racial ghetto a destructive environment totally unknown to most white Americans," the report read. "What white Americans have never fully understood—but what the Negro can never forget—is that white society is deeply implicated in the ghetto. White institutions created it, white institutions maintain it, and white society condones it."

After the 1968 riots, unscrupulous realtors in Chicago played upon the fears of white homeowners, convincing them to sell quickly and cheaply. Most white residents took the bait, and before long most of the remaining west side "flipped" and became almost entirely African-American, deflating the prospect of integrated neighborhoods. Economically, the west side never fully recovered from the 1968 riots. Most white merchants burned from their stores didn't return, and more than three decades later, vacant lots still dot the Madison Street landscape where a thriving business district once existed.

It is indeed ironic that the life of a man who advocated nonviolence in his attempts to bring equality to all Americans would be brought down by violence. Dr. Martin Luther King, Jr. changed the world far beyond the power of hatred to rescind, and his loss is said to be everyone's loss. But not only was a man of peace killed that April week in 1968; on the west side of Chicago, a neighborhood died with him.

The 1960s saw many of Chicago's older industrial buildings fall to fire.
Here an abandoned factory at Harrison and Throop Streets burns in 1967.

The City That Works

For more than a century, Chicago has experienced more than its share of industrial mishaps. One of the worst occurred January 20, 1909. The location was not a dangerous factory building or slaughterhouse but rather a water crib in Lake Michigan a mile and a half off shore. The culprit in this instance? Fire.

Ever since Chicago was a small village, it has drawn water from Lake Michigan. As the population grew, a better system was necessary to supply its inhabitants with the requisite volume of water that was colorless, odorless, tasteless, and free of bacterial impurities. In 1867, pipes were extended beneath the lakebed to intake cribs erected two to four miles from shore. As the city's demand for water increased, more cribs were built to meet the need.

In January 1909, construction was under way on one such crib located in the lake about two miles off 70th Street. The crib sat above a water intake port that was at the end of a 12,000-foot-long tunnel being extended under the lakebed from shore. A second temporary crib was located about a half mile in from the permanent crib. This second crib was used to house workers and equipment and also to protect the 180-foot digging shaft that extended from the surface down into the bedrock. During the winter months, workers digging the tunnel lived aboard the 88-foot-wide wooden crib, working round the clock on three shifts. Though strong enough to withstand storms and ice, the crib was by no means a safe place. It was built entirely of wood and had no lifeboats moored to it. Personnel were housed there not as a convenience to them but to ensure that work could be carried out during the winter without disruption. To maintain communication with shore, telephone lines were run across the water on a steel aerial tramway.

On the morning of January 20, between 79 and 100 workers were aboard the crib when, around 8 o'clock, a fire broke out in the dining room and spread so fast that within minutes the entire structure was engulfed in flames. The fire erupted as the midnight shift was being relieved; most workers were on the second floor of the crib, and many were changing their clothes. They were caught off guard and became trapped and burned. "The crib is on fire . . . For God's sake send help," screamed one worker who made a half-finished call from the burning crib to its headquarters in the Jackson Tunneling Company

A deceptively idyllic wintertime scene showing
ice-encrusted fire apparatus during a 1950s blaze.

the water. In the crib, half-naked workers fought to free themselves. But the crib had only nine windows and three exit doors, each of which soon became jammed with bodies of men clawing and fighting each other for a chance to jump into the frigid lake, even if it meant drowning. A number of them did manage to save themselves this way, floating on large pieces of ice or by reaching a dump pile of mud and muck that extended a few feet above the water's surface. But most workers had been unable to escape the fire's grip and were incinerated as a result, many while sleeping in bunks arranged around the crib's wooden walls. The tugboat *T.T. Morford* was tied up at the 68th Street crib a half mile away. "Cast off," ordered its captain, A.E. Johnson, who saw the fire from the tug's bridge. When the *Morford* pulled up to the crib several minutes later, its crew began picking up survivors and bodies. It was soon joined by two other tugs. Together they made several trips to shore. Fireboats arrived and hosed water on the burning structure until the flames subsided. Then firefighters boarded it to begin taking out the dead. Forty-eight bodies were recovered. Another 12 men had drowned in the water before being reached. When the last of the flames were doused, the crib resembled a huge box of splintered matchsticks. Only one man was discovered alive, having found refuge by climbing down the tunnel shaft.

At the time of the fire, about 300 pounds of dynamite, enough for one day's blasting and digging, had been stored in the crib in a first floor powder room. Officials agreed it burned without exploding because no one reported hearing or seeing a blast. According to the city engineer's report, the crib was equipped with two fire pumps fitted with hose, but neither was used, probably because of panic and the swiftness of the flames. As for what caused the blaze, a definitive answer was never given, although two theories were investigated. One said that a

terminus on shore.[1] Before the call could be completed, the caller was cut off when flames severed the telephone line from the tramway.

The fire raged, fed by a strong south wind that blew across

Snorkels set up to wage battle as flames devour a huge grain elevator along the Chicago River at 32nd Street in 1966.

Smoke and flames billow from Chicago's Union Station during a 1980 fire that left one man dead.

Flames pour from the top of a factory in Old Town that had been converted into a huge art gallery. The April 1989 blaze destroyed the entire structure as well as millions of dollars of artwork.

worker tried to kill rodents by pouring gasoline into cracks at several points inside the crib's structure, and that it somehow ignited. A second alleged that another worker was seen entering the powder room with a lighted torch. Both accounts were unfounded.

The final death toll was never fixed. Varying reports placed the count between 60 and 70. All were men and many had families; most were European immigrants or African-Americans from the South. Three days after the disaster, a large funeral attended by thousands was held in the South Chicago neighborhood, where neighborhood factories closed and church bells tolled. The funeral cortege proceeded from St. Patrick's Church to Mount Greenwood Cemetery, where the victims were laid to rest in a mass grave on top of which was placed a memorial marking their passage in one of Chicago's worst and least-remembered tragedies.

ON MAY 11, 1939, Chicago experienced another massive workplace fire, this one after exploding grain dust sparked a blaze that destroyed five large grain elevators belonging to the Rosenbaum and Norris Grain Company. The huge ten-story elevators were part of a vast complex of buildings along the western bank of the Calumet River between 102nd and 103rd Streets. Before it burned itself out, the fire killed nine workers and caused nearly $4 million in damage. More than 4 million bushels of grain were lost, causing grain prices to shoot up for a time on the Chicago commodities and futures exchange. The fire, one of Chicago's largest, required a response of more than

An abandoned building burns in 1982 in the South Loop.

500 firefighters utilizing 62 land companies and two fireboats. Radiant heat blistered paint on several fire apparatus and damaged several thousand of feet of hose.

The Rosenbaum fire would not be the last deadly Chicago fire caused by dust particles exploding, a hazard now strictly regulated by federal and state occupational safety agencies. On September 7, 1948, corn dust or starch used in the manufacture of candy ignited in the Brach's Candy factory at 4656 W. Kinzie St., causing a violent blast despite the presence of an air ventilation system designed to prevent such an occurrence. About 35 men were reporting for work when the explosion rocked the plant at 4 A.M. Eleven were killed and ten others were injured.

The same thing happened five years later when an electronics plant on the city's north side blew up suddenly without warning, killing 35 workers. The Haber Corporation at 908 W. North Ave., a manufacturer of electronics and aircraft parts, was owned and operated by Titus Haffa, a former Chicago alderman who in 1930 was sentenced to a 17-month jail term for violating Prohibition laws. After leaving prison, Haffa opened his plant and, in the years following World War II, employed many immigrants.

For the 100 men and women working on April 14, 1953, the morning had begun unremarkably at the Haber plant. Located in an industrial district near the intersection of North and Clybourn Avenues, the four-story factory had been built in 1882 and was undergoing an extensive remodeling. As a result, one of its three interior stairways had been boarded up, and the outside fire escape landing on the third floor was removed. The building was otherwise in good shape, with fire doors and an operable sprinkler system. But whatever safety devices were in place that morning didn't matter because at exactly 8:41 A.M., a large section of the building blew apart when a high concentra-tion of flammable particle dust ignited in a third-floor assembly room. The massive explosion rocked the entire neighborhood, hurtling bricks and debris in all directions and rattling windows on buildings several blocks away. It was followed by several secondary blasts that tore through the building and knocked out the sprinkler system. Flames from the erupting fireballs spread quickly throughout the plant's third and fourth floors, burning through the roof and sending a column of smoke visible nearly two miles away.

The third floor was quickly destroyed. Several employees working in the immediate blast area died instantly. Other panic-stricken workers ran about the building with their hair and clothing aflame, rushing windows and doors in search of escape. Several were trampled and more were injured when they jumped from second and third floor windows, some landing on a neighboring rooftop 14 feet below. The jumpers were forced to do so because of the missing fire escape and the closed stairway.

The first alarm reporting the blast was received at 8:47 A.M., and in less than 15 minutes, a 5-11 alarm was sounded, bringing a third of Chicago's on-duty firefighting force to the scene. The initial priority for firefighters was life safety, but before they could enter the building they first had to contain the fire. Compounding the situation was a 35-m.p.h. wind that increased the flames. Firefighters poured water into the factory for more than two hours before bringing the fire under control. Rescuers then began digging through the rubble in search of survivors. Instead they recovered 35 bodies.

In a scene repeated many times throughout Chicago's history, grieving relatives filed into the basement of the Cook County morgue to identify the remains of the victims. "She was my mother," one man told a morgue attendant as a sheet was pulled back to reveal a woman's burned body.[2] For others it was a daughter, a son, a husband, a wife. One man who emerged from the morgue wiping his eyes was 46 and a native of Austria. His wife had died in the same Yugoslav prison camp from which he had escaped in 1945. After the war, he immigrated to Chicago with his two young daughters. Now one of them, a 17-year-old, had become the Haber blast's youngest victim. Another victim was a Puerto Rican immigrant who had worked at the plant for 18 months until finally saving enough money to send for his wife and three children. They had been scheduled to arrive in Chicago the following week. Now they wouldn't be coming at all.

The explosion was eventually ruled an accident and attributed to a blower-type exhaust system that had failed to remove flammable dust particles gathering inside the plant. It was touched off when the dust contacted either sparks from a metal polishing machine or static electricity. One day after the tragedy, owner Haffa vowed to erect a memorial park on the factory site. The park never materialized and nothing was ever done to commemorate the fire. Today the once industrial North and Clybourn neighborhood is largely gentrified, its factories having either burned down or replaced by a suburban-looking shopping district. Occupying the site where the 35 workers lost their lives is an awkward structure reminiscent of a large kitchen appliance. It houses an upscale home store.

Firefighters battle a stubborn tenement fire on Milwaukee Avenue in 1965. Residential blazes kill more Americans than all natural disasters combined and account for more than 80 percent of annual fire deaths.

Home Fires Burning

The cliché that a man's home is his castle is not quite so matter-of-fact when one realizes that the home is the one place in America where death by fire is most likely to occur.

Fires kill about 3,600 Americans each year, roughly one every two and a half hours. And someone is injured in a fire every 24 minutes. A fire is reported every 17 seconds and breaks out in the home every 85 seconds. Residential blazes comprise 70 percent of all reported structure fires and cause 80 percent of all fire fatalities, making fire the third leading cause of accidental death in the home. Most residential fires occur between the hours of 2 A.M. and 6 A.M. when most people are in bed. And even though smoke detectors have greatly reduced the number of fire deaths overall, firefighters are still called to extinguish fatal home fires in which smoke detectors were either absent or not working.

Like most big cities, Chicago has experienced its share of deadly residential fires. Fires in single-family homes as well as in apartment buildings, hotels, nursing homes, and a host of other institutions have taken an enormous human toll. In researching Chicago's fire history, it is not uncommon to find innumerable instances in which one blaze, whether in a single-family dwelling or an apartment building, claimed several lives, sometimes up to 11 at a time. The circumstances and causes of these multi-death fires vary, but invariably poverty, overcrowding, and poor housekeeping figure prominently. This is not to suggest that fire discriminates, for certainly it does not; its deadly effects reach into affluent neighborhoods just as easily as in the lowest of ghettos. But the poor are far more likely to be victimized by fire than the wealthy.

An example of the dangerous liaison between poverty, overcrowding, and fire occurred early on September 7, 1953, when 18 people fell victim to a fire in a slum apartment building at 3616 S. State St., in the heart of the so-called Black Belt. The area contained some of the worst housing in the nation, with many dwellings lacking running water or heat. This building was no exception. Built in 1890, the 63-year-old, four-story tenement was in deplorable condition. And though its outer walls were brick, its interior was almost entirely wood, lathe, and plaster, and included many hollow core walls. The top three floors contained apartments, while the first floor was occupied by a storefront saloon. The building had three

(*Left*) An elderly victim of the Wincrest Nursing Home is removed by a rescuer during the smoky January 30, 1976, arson fire that left 24 dead. (*Right*) Technology vs. Nature: Even the most sophisticated equipment is no match for the formidable foe of flames.

stairways: an open wooden staircase running through the center of its interior, an outside front fire escape, and an exterior wooden stairway connected to rear porches. Rats, roaches, and bad electrical wiring combined to make living conditions primitively grim as did the absence of a central boiler to provide heat or hot water. Consequently, during the harsh winter months, tenants had to warm their apartments with individual gas stoves or oil burners. And like so many other multi-family tenements in the area, the building was severely overcrowded—about 150 men, women, and children lived there. These circumstances allowed 3616 S. State to deliver on its promise of being a terrible firetrap destined to make headlines.

At around two in the morning, Mrs. Alma Cantrell, operator of the saloon on the first floor, closed up and retired to her living quarters directly behind the bar. A few patrons remained, drinking with the bartender who was cleaning up. Cantrell was falling asleep when she heard shouting. Someone banged on her door. "Get up," the bartender yelled to her. "The building's on fire."[1]

She threw on her bathrobe and ran into the bar, escaping with the others through the front door. Meanwhile, heat from the fire had shattered the rear windows, enabling it to spread rapidly up the rear wooden stairway, cutting off escape for scores of tenants whose apartments were directly above. The fire quickly grew as it raced up the back stairway, breaking windows and entering the rear apartments, feeding on rickety wooden construction and an abundant supply of combustibles and furnishings. It reached the fourth floor and broke through the roof, shooting flames fifty feet into the morning sky.

In the era before smoke detectors, shouts of warning and panic roused the sleeping tenants who awoke in the smoky darkness. With children in tow, they ran through the smoke-dense hallways in search of a way out. With the rear stairway cut off by the fire, many tenants sought escape down the interior stairway and front fire escape. But other people found themselves blocked. Unable to reach the front of the building, they started hanging from the upper windows and dropping to the ground. Several suffered broken limbs, but some were lucky enough to break their falls by landing on an adjacent shanty in the back alley. Others unable to make it to the windows became trapped and died.

In no time the entire 125-foot-long building was an inferno. The fire department arrived quickly, but 20 minutes after the first engine pulled up, the rear two-thirds of the building collapsed into the basement. The fire also swept into the upper floors of the two adjacent structures. Firefighters worked for more than two hours to bring the flames under control. Several more hours would pass before the victims were located. Bulldozers and cranes were called in to knock down the remaining walls in aid of the search. By the next day, firefighters had recovered 18 bodies: five women, four men, and nine children. Nine of the victims were discovered huddled together in one room in a single third-floor apartment, all from the same family.

Though the official cause of the fire was never determined, investigators theorized that either exposed electrical wiring or a discarded cigarette was responsible. Cantrell, the tavern owner, survived the fire. And even though it began in the rear of her apartment on the first floor, there was no evidence that she or the bar patrons were responsible. No one was ever prosecuted, despite the building being maintained by a real estate firm listed as one of Chicago's principal slum operators.

The death trap was never rebuilt. Eventually the other tenements on State Street were razed as part of urban renewal begun in the mid-1950s. Unfortunately, this case of urban

Fire consumes a building containing stores and apartments at Harrison and Western in 1962. This scene was oft-repeated in Chicago in the 1960s and 1970s, as once thriving neighborhoods fell into disrepair.

renewal didn't result in urban rebirth. Today the area remains as blighted as ever, occupied by an even bigger slum—the Robert Taylor Homes, the largest and arguably most dangerous public housing project in the United States. Opened in 1962 as a stopping off point for working class families on their way to a better life, the complex of imposing high rises instead became a point of no return for a perpetual black underclass unable to escape the snare of its concrete ghetto. As this book is being written, the Robert Taylor homes have been partially razed, its entire destruction slated for 2001.

NOT EVERYONE lives in a house or an apartment building. Many people reside in college dormitories, hotels, military barracks, orphanages, and other institutions, such as hospitals, nursing homes, and various extended-care facilities. Fires in these have a greater potential for disaster because of the high concentration of residents in a single structure. This hazard is worsened considerably whenever the residents have special needs.

Officially, the former tuberculosis pavilion at Chicago's Dunning Asylum for the Insane was called Annex No. One. Unofficially, the hospital barracks was known more familiarly by two other names: the "Cigar Box," due to its wooden construction, and the "Death House," because it housed supposedly incurable cases. Both would eventually prove true because, on the day after Christmas in 1923, the building burned like a giant matchbox, killing 19.

The Dunning Asylum, later renamed Chicago State Hospital, and finally the Chicago-Read Mental Health Center, was a sprawling medical complex on a large plot of state-owned land along Irving Park Road on the city's far northwest side. Built after the Civil War, it had once been the site of the Cook County Poor Farm. A potter's field there contained unmarked pauper's graves as well as the unidentified remains of numerous victims killed in the Great Chicago Fire.

Annex No. One, built in 1903, had become antiquated and unfit for use by 1923. Separate from the main hospital, the wooden double H-shaped structure had six wards connected by a common corridor. Two of its wings were two stories high while the remaining four wings, including the dining hall, were one story. It had no sprinkler system and all the exit doors opened inward against state fire laws. The building nevertheless housed 388 patients, many of whom had been admitted involuntarily because they were violent, disturbed, or both.

At 5:30 P.M. on December 26, 1923, the patients were eating dinner in the dining hall, an independent wing of the barracks that jutted from the main living quarters. A post-Christmas celebration was scheduled to begin soon. One young man who had finished eating early returned to his room in Ward Three to say prayers. As he knelt next to his cot, flames suddenly erupted from a wooden clothes closet. In a panic he ran back to the dining hall screaming, "fire, fire, fire."

The fire quickly spread from the room to the wooden corridor. Aided by an abundance of oxygen and combustibles that included the varnished wooden floors coated with numerous layers of flammable wax, it soon engulfed the entire building, finally reaching the crowded dining room filled with hundreds of now-hysterical mentally ill patients.

Across Irving Park Road, the owner of an auto mechanic's shop heard the shouting, saw the fire, and called the fire department. Someone started banging the alarm bell on the asylum grounds to notify the hospital's private fire brigade. Units from the brigade arrived first, followed shortly by the Chicago Fire Department. Firefighters from both crews were familiar with the sprawling complex because during the past 13 years, eight fires had erupted on the site, including fires in dormitories and horse barns, though with no loss of life. But this time firefighters would face catastrophe.

The first priority of the firefighters was life safety, but in order to enter the building and effect rescue, they had to subdue the flames shooting from every window. Fortunately, their job was made a little easier by the quick actions of hospital workers, nurses, and security guards, who, despite the panic, led several hundred patients away from the fire. Police had also chopped down a door to rescue three occupants who locked themselves in a bathroom. Sixteen other patients were less fortunate. Unable to escape the dining hall, they burned to death. Several were found stacked up against inward-opening exit doors. Three others, a man, his wife, and their 13-year-old son, had also had perished in the fire. The man worked as a hospital clerk, his wife a laundress. All three had been attending the party and reportedly escaped the fire only to return to retrieve trunks containing their belongings.

The confusion enabled a number of inmates to slip away from the asylum. All across Chicago, police were alerted with orders to round them up. About 50 of the escapees were eventually located, many along skid row on west Madison Street. Others turned themselves in at local police stations after wandering the streets for hours.

After the annex fire was extinguished, fire officials combed the wreckage in search of a cause. Three possibilities emerged: spontaneous combustion; careless smoking; or, as reported in a *Chicago Daily News* story that represents the colorful and often cavalier writing style of the era, "that one of the demented inmates may have attempted suicide by locking himself in a closet and setting himself on fire."[2] As it turned out, no official cause was ever determined, though investigators later felt certain the fire started after a patient or attendant carelessly discarded a cigar or cigarette in the closet, allowing it

to smolder. Like all such tragedies before and since, the Dunning fire resulted in calls for stricter fire regulations and inspections.

HISTORY TEACHES us that no one is immune from fire. Some, however, such as children and the elderly, are more susceptible to its hazards. An example occurred January 30, 1976, when a relatively small but deadly fire broke out on the top floor of the Wincrest Nursing Home at 6326 N. Winthrop Ave. on Chicago's far north side. Only a few blocks from Lake Michigan, the four-story, 88-room intermediate care facility was home to 83 residents whose average age was 87 years.

Shortly before noon, a missionary priest was ending the daily Catholic mass in the top floor chapel when a nurse's aid ran up to him and announced, "Father, there's a fire and it's serious."[3]

The priest left to investigate and spotted a fire in Room 306, about 20 feet down the corridor. Another nurse who had followed him pulled the fire alarm and then began evacuating residents from their rooms. A maintenance worker and an administrator joined the priest and tried to douse the flames with portable water fire extinguishers they had grabbed from the walls. Flames shot to the ceiling while the smoke turned darker and banked to the floor, making it impossible to breathe. The fire was burning inside a large wooden clothes wardrobe on the far wall of the room and was spreading to the draperies, furniture, and four mattresses, creating untenable heat and smoke that drove the staff back. They retreated to the chapel, but in their haste failed to close the door to the burning room, allowing the heavy black smoke to pour into the corridor. Within seconds the smoke began swirling into the chapel where between 30 and 40 mostly elderly women were seated in wooden pews or confined to wheelchairs. Another nine residents were stuck inside their rooms. All were about to be overcome by toxic smoke.

The Chicago Fire Department was automatically notified of the fire at 11:43 A.M., after the nurse pulled the fire alarm. The fire also triggered heat detectors inside the nursing home connected directly to the fire alarm system. A box alarm assignment was immediately transmitted by the city's main fire alarm office, sending four engines, two hook-and-ladders, a flying squad, a snorkel, one divisional marshal, and two battalion chiefs, a force of 39 in all. Hook-and-Ladder 47 was the first to arrive, within three minutes of the initial alarm. Wearing self-contained breathing apparatus, the firefighters raced up the stairs to the top floor, then felt their way along the walls in the blinding smoke. They found elderly residents either gasping for breath or already slumped over unconscious in their wheelchairs in the chapel. Needing help to remove the victims, they placed a special call for three additional flying squads. Three minutes later a 2-11 alarm was transmitted. The city's disaster plan alerting all area hospitals and social service agencies was also put in effect.

Even though the firefighters were able to stretch hoselines and put out the fire relatively quickly, the effects of the smoke had been deadly. Because many of the elderly residents were overcome or otherwise unable to escape without help, rescuers had to carry them down the four flights of stairs. In the narrow alley behind the nursing home, ambulances and police squadrols lined up to take dozens of victims to one of four local hospitals. Thirteen were listed as being dead on arrival. Eleven more would succumb within a few hours or a few days. The

dead ranged in age from 46 to 94. All but two had been inside the chapel, and all but one was female. Each had died from smoke inhalation. Thirty others had been injured and required hospitalization, including several staff members, police officers, and firefighters.

Built in 1953, the Wincrest had been extensively remodeled in 1960 and again in 1973. It was a modern, well-maintained

Fire apparatus along Washington Boulevard following a fire in an abandoned west side tenement, 1990.

facility and had received no major health, fire, or building code violations. The building featured mostly fire-resistive construction, had enclosed stairwells, and was equipped throughout with heat and smoke detectors. Yet the Wincrest did not have a sprinkler system because the law didn't require it. Had one been in place, it would have easily put out the fire in its early phase, keeping it confined to Room 306. Instead the room was completely gutted; the corridor sustained moderate fire and intense smoke damage; and three neighboring rooms whose doors had been left open suffered moderate heat and smoke damage. The floor's remaining four rooms were undamaged because their doors were closed. A special panel convened by Mayor Richard J. Daley to investigate the fire recommended several changes to the city's fire codes, including installation of sprinkler systems in all new and existing nursing homes. Also suggested was the connection of sprinkler water flow alarms to the fire department's alarm receiving system.

How did the fire start? Like all fire investigations, a process of elimination began, and after quickly dismissing the heating and electrical systems as likely causes, investigators looked at circumstances that pointed to arson. The first concerned the fire's sudden eruption and intense burning inside an unoccupied room. At the time of the fire, the room's occupants were inside the chapel attending mass. After conducting interviews with staff and residents, investigators focused on a 21-year-old female housekeeper who had been a suspect in a number of other unrelated arson cases. Initially, the woman told police she entered Room 306 to clean it and had started the fire accidentally while using a match to search in the dark for something. But when police pressed her, the woman broke down and admitted to setting the fire intentionally by igniting a pile of clothes inside the wooden wardrobe. She was charged and eventually convicted of multiple counts of murder and arson. Though her motive remained vague, her fetish for starting fires assured the Wincrest an unenviable place in history, making it one of America's deadliest nursing home fires.

Working in frigid temperatures, firefighters search for three comrades killed in a February 1985 arson fire on the northwest side.

In the Line of Duty

Each year in the United States, more firefighters per capita die or become injured in the line of duty than do miners, police officers, or construction workers—about 100 annually—making firefighting arguably America's most dangerous non-military profession. Advances in safety and technology have lowered these numbers; nevertheless, the work of a firefighter remains dirty, dangerous, and sometimes deadly. And though some may wax poetic about the subject, labeling a firefighter's death the "ultimate sacrifice," the reality is quite different. When a firefighter is killed, there is nothing poetic or gallant about it. Rather it is usually a violent, horrible death, the result of an accident, a mistake or misjudgment, a faulty piece of protective equipment, or an unseen hazard. If it occurs during an arson fire, it's murder. Regardless of the circumstances, once the funerals have ended, with their bagpipes, eulogies, and inevitable speeches by politicians, what remains for grieving family members are empty holidays, uncertain futures, and unending thoughts of what might have been.

The city of Chicago has proven to be one of the deadliest in which to be a firefighter. As of this writing, 551 Chicago firefighters have been killed since the paid fire department was formed in 1858. It is a sobering statistic, one that, unfortunately and inevitably, will increase with time.

The first two firefighters in Chicago to lay down their lives were pipemen Ignatz Geiss of Engine 9 and John Trainor of Engine 5. Both were killed June 7, 1865, when a wall collapsed on them during a stubborn warehouse fire at 185 S. Water St., a blaze that left another 18 firefighters injured. Exactly one year later, on June 7, 1866, firefighter Daniel Heart of Engine 8 became the third to lose his life when the apparatus on which he was riding collided with a train while responding to a fire on LaSalle Street. Eight more would die before the close of the 1860s: Michael Burns, assigned to Hook-and-Ladder 9, suffocated April 13, 1867, when fire swept a building on Wabash Avenue. Less than one month later, on May 4, 1867, two firefighters from Engine 10 and one from Engine 1 were lost in a fire at 89 S. Water St. Another four men died March 5, 1869, while battling a mill fire on Canal Street.

Firefighting in the nineteenth century was crude, primitive, and very labor intensive. And though the industrial age introduced mechanization and widespread manufacturing, it also brought increased complexities to firefighting. Structures were

(*Left*) Ice blankets firefighters and equipment following the huge fire at the Hilker-Bletsch warehouse in January 1961. Nine firefighters were killed when the building collapsed. (*Right*) Civilians come to the aid of a firefighter injured during the February 1968 blast at the Mickelberry sausage plant. Nine people, including four firefighters, were killed when a gasoline truck exploded.

thrown up cheaply and quickly, and there were few building codes governing their construction. As factories grew in size and office and mercantile buildings began rising higher, fire equipment remained horse-drawn and manually operated. And though no firefighters died in the Great Chicago Fire of 1871, 73 did die between 1875 and 1900, a period coinciding with enormous growth and prosperity for Chicago.

The arrival of the twentieth century didn't make firefighting any easier or safer. On January 9, 1918, six men died fighting a blaze in a dilapidated theater on the city's west side. Flames had erupted inside the building on Chicago Avenue near Leavitt Street shortly before midnight. Blowing winds created snowdrifts several feet high that severely hampered firefighters' attempts to stretch hoselines. These delays enabled the blaze to spread rapidly throughout the three-story building, engulfing the unoccupied dance floor and clubrooms. Eventually flames burned through the roof.

Firefighters endured for several hours in the icy darkness, braving frigid temperatures and playing thousands of gallons of water into the blazing theater. John Davey had been among the first to arrive, and he and his company had taken a severe beating. Davey was operating a hose in front of the burning building when another firefighter, Peter Horan, walked over to relieve him. "Let me have the pipe, Jack." Horan said. "You're tired." The shivering Davey relented, handing over the nozzle and the coveted position at the front of the hose line. "Okay," he replied. "But I'll be back."[1]

As Davey trudged in his boots through the knee-deep snow, he spotted other firefighters entering a neighboring building to warm up. Davey had traveled only a few steps when a sudden crash caused him to stop. Tons of snow on the theater rooftop had conspired with the weakening effects of the fire and the application of heavy water streams to undermine the building's structural supports, causing its entire front wall and large electric marquee to come crashing down onto a group of firefighters working directly beneath. Davey and the others quickly forgot the cold and instead climbed onto the mountain of broken debris to begin digging out their comrades. Eventually the remains of four firefighters were recovered. One of the bodies was Peter Horan. Another injured firefighter died two days later on the eve of what would have been his first wedding anniversary, while yet another succumbed to his injuries ten months later.

On April 14, 1931, four firefighters were among the 12 people killed after a flash fire erupted inside a sanitary district deep tunnel near 22nd Street and Laflin Avenue. The firefighters, one captain, one lieutenant, and two firemen, had descended into the tunnel to save workers overcome by smoke and fumes. Sixteen sanitary workers were eventually rescued from the pit. The fire originated when a workman's candle ignited sawdust on the tunnel floor. Before the flames could be fully extinguished and the remaining workers rescued, however, a special smoke ejector had to be brought in from Kenosha, Wisconsin, to clear the tunnel.

On August 17, 1940, a 2-11 alarm fire inside the Van Schaack Bros. chemical works at 3420 W. Henderson Ave. on Chicago's northwest side began as a relatively routine incident. Firefighters quashed the fire fairly quickly. But tragedy struck without warning when, as they went about picking up their hoselines between two sections of the two-story brick building, a large tank of flammable benzol suddenly exploded, enveloping them in a huge sheet of flame. Two lieutenants and two firemen were killed instantly. Another firefighter died three days later from severe burns. Officials suspected that a

The leveled main section of the Mickelberry plant.

spark from a bursting light bulb triggered the blast.

An even greater tragedy occurred three years later. At around 8:30 P.M. on the mild Thursday evening of July 9, 1943, an alarm was received for a fire at 419 W. Superior St. after flames were discovered burning on the second floor of the four-story warehouse west of downtown. The blaze was quickly extinguished and fire crews returned to their quarters. But at 2 A.M. the fire rekindled and fire companies were called back. This time flames were burning fiercely throughout the building's top floor, where a model airplane company kept hundreds of cardboard storage cartons stacked to the ceiling. The fire was soon raised to four alarms, bringing 30 fire companies and 160 men. Firefighters attacked the flames from the outside, utilizing powerful master streams from water towers and deluge pipes. But to reach the seat of the fire, they also had to make their way inside the building with handlines. About 20 men were stretching a hose up the front stairway to the fourth floor when the roof and part of the front wall suddenly failed, sending the entire front part of the building— including the stairway on which the firemen were standing— into the basement. The men had plunged down as many as three flights of stairs before becoming entombed under tons of bricks, concrete, and heavy timber. Some were crushed to death instantly. Others remained trapped for up to 11 hours. "I thought the noise of the falling bricks would never stop," recalled one chief whose false teeth had been broken by the shattering crash.[2]

Tedious rescue work proceeded throughout that morning. Initially the bodies of two firefighters were pulled through a manhole cover in the street directly outside the wrecked building. But to reach the remaining men, air hammers were brought in to punch through the 18-inch concrete walls of an adjacent building. As the precarious work of tunneling into the wreckage droned on, a fire department physician crawled into the bowels of the destruction to administer morphine to several trapped firefighters who writhed in pain. Monsignor William J. Gorman, the fire department's chaplain, accompanied him to help ease fears. At one point, Gorman urged one of the firefighters, Lt. Richard Jablonski of Truck 2, to say an Act of Contrition. "Father," replied the injured firefighter, "I've said it a thousand times since we've been here."[3] Jablonski died later from his injuries.

Though it was never determined how the blaze started, officials attributed the collapse to the extraordinary weight created when thousands of gallons of water were poured onto the fire. The water had doused the flames, but it had also soaked and weighed down the hundreds of cardboard boxes stored on the building's top floor. When the floors could no longer support this added weight, they failed, sending three captains, one lieutenant, and four firefighters to their deaths.

MOST OF the city's population was asleep during the bitterly cold early morning hours of December 17, 1953. This included the 70 or so residents of the Reliance Hotel, a 50-cent flophouse at 1700 W. Madison St. Located west of the Loop and one block east of the Chicago Stadium, the Reliance was built in 1885 and had 45 rooms, 17 on the second floor and 28 on the third. The hotel office, a small meat market, and a drug store shared the first floor. Like many buildings on skid row, the Reliance was a firetrap; despite being a public occupancy, it was without a sprinkler system or fire alarm and most of its interior was built entirely of wood. What's more, all of its stairways were open, which in the event of a fire, provided an unobstructed means for smoke and flames to spread quickly through the structure. This is precisely what occurred when, at

Mourners, including Chicago Mayor Harold Washington and Fire Commissioner Louis T. Galante, greet a casket as it enters Holy Name Cathedral following the death of three firefighters in February 1985.

around 2:20 A.M., a fire erupted in the center of the building. After noticing smoke, the hotel manager first phoned the fire department, then began knocking on doors to rouse the sleeping residents. Meanwhile, two police officers in a passing patrol car also noticed smoke issuing from the hotel and radioed for help. The fire department responded quickly. But for five firefighters, it would be their last alarm.

People were already fleeing into the street when the first fire companies arrived. In their haste, many residents had run into the frigid night wearing just undergarments and blankets. Three alarms were sounded, bringing enough firefighters to both rescue occupants and fight the smoky fire, a task that took about an hour to accomplish. Afterward, they continued working inside the building, conducting a final search for any hidden pockets of fire and for any victims. It was then that a steel roof beam suddenly slipped out of place, bringing down the entire front center of the building. In a repeat of earlier tragedies, the debris pancaked into the basement, burying the unsuspecting firefighters beneath tons of broken concrete and heavy timbers.

Five men on the roof had been lucky: they managed to ride down the collapsing rooftop, narrowly escaping serious injury. Though cut and bruised, they crawled to safety. But those inside the building were less fortunate. They became imprisoned beneath tons of bricks, lumber, steel, bedding, furniture, and other heavy debris. With the sound of crashing walls still ringing in their ears, about 100 firefighters began digging in the ruins to reach those stuck inside. Guided by floodlights, they clawed their way through the wreckage using axes, saws, shovels, and bare hands. A few of the men were able to free themselves. But 14 others remained pinned inside the rubble, some conscious and yelling for help. Those unable to move pleaded for rescue and prayed aloud. "We're praying too and working to get you out," one rescuer shouted back. "Just keep praying."[4]

Three physicians summoned to the hotel crawled inside to administer morphine to a few of the injured firemen waiting for rescue, injecting limbs sticking out of the wreckage. Even with a section of the rooftop hanging precariously overhead, the rescuers continued digging in the freezing temperatures, removing debris with bare, bloodied hands. One by one the trapped firefighters were located and carried away. Injuries included fractured bones, bruises, cuts, and smoke inhalation. The bodies of three firefighters had also been located and removed. But two were still missing, and as daylight arrived, hope dimmed. Fearing a secondary collapse, Fire Commissioner Anthony Mullaney ordered all firefighters from the wreckage. Ten minutes later, a large portion of the overhanging roof broke away and fell into the basement in the exact spot where many rescuers had just been working. A crane with a large shovel was brought in to sift the ruins. Before long another body was located in the basement, that of acting Lieutenant George Malik of Engine Co. 34. All that morning, Malik's wife, Julia, her hands clutching a pair of rosary beads, had maintained a hopeful vigil in a fire chief's car parked outside the smashed hotel. But upon witnessing her 37-year-old husband's peril, she turned hysterical and had to be led away. Malik's father, a retired postal worker, stood alongside tearful firefighters who bowed their heads as his son's body was carried out. The last body was recovered at 5 P.M., more than 12 hours after the collapse.[5]

The lone civilian killed in the fire was a 39-year-old Chicago man who had checked into the Reliance following his release the day before from a state mental hospital in southern Illinois, where over the years he had served five separate stays. Firefighters had located his body in the basement, near the spot

One Chicago firefighter was killed during this New Year's Eve fire on north Clark Street in 1968.

where the fire had originated. On the night of the fire, the man had reportedly left the hotel at 10 P.M., returning about 2 A.M. The blaze was discovered about 20 minutes later. A handwritten note found on his body and scribbled on a cigarette pack described numerous crimes he had allegedly committed, including murder, rape, and arson. But when police checked his background, they found no record indicating he had committed any of the crimes mentioned. Police surmised someone else had written the note, especially after the man's family adamantly denied that he had ever started any previous fires or had a history of violence. Police investigated one other suspect who confessed to starting the fire, but this claim was also unfounded. Poor housekeeping was eventually deemed the fire's most likely cause.

As for what triggered the building to collapse, it was determined that a large steel "I" beam had slipped out of its base after rapidly expanding from the heat of the fire and then quickly cooling and contracting when the blaze was extinguished. But because it had not been permanently fastened to the building by rivets or other means (building codes at the time of the Reliance's construction in 1885 didn't require it), the beam twisted and fell out of place, causing the entire building to topple.

THE 1960s debuted in Chicago by repeating history in the form of dead firefighters, grieving widows, and fatherless children. In the first year of the new decade, 18 more firefighters would answer their final alarm, half in a single recurrence of past tragedies.

At 6:23 on the morning of January 28, 1961, two Chicago police officers on routine patrol radioed their headquarters that the building at Hubbard and Jefferson Streets was on fire. At about the same time, a city transit dispatcher who also noticed the blaze from his office window in the nearby Merchandise Mart telephoned the fire department to say the fire was "going like hell." This prompted fire alarm operators to tap out Box 286, bringing a full response of fire equipment.

Burning was the huge Hilker-Bletsch baking supply company at 614 W. Hubbard St., a seven-story building in a densely-built industrial district west of downtown and directly north of an elevated railroad viaduct. When firefighters arrived, flames were already roaring throughout the entire ground floor of the structure, the fire fueled by a variety of combustibles as well as an ample supply of cooking and baking fats. Conditions deteriorated quickly and the fire soon overtook the entire front or east side of the building, spreading to all seven floors and the roof. Five more alarms were sounded, bringing an armada of firefighters and equipment to the scene. But even this couldn't fend off the disaster that was about to occur.

Because the burning building was beyond saving, fire officials turned to a defensive operation to prevent the huge blaze from spreading into adjacent two- and three-story brick structures. Chief George Kuhn of the 5th Battalion led a group of firefighters into the two-story property north of the fire while another company of firefighters led by 1st Battalion Chief George Rees was sent to check conditions in the three-story building to the south. By this time the entire Hilker-Bletsch building had burst into a mass of flames, creating a dangerous collapse hazard. Just as firefighters searching the two exposed structures were ordered to withdraw, a portion of the building's southeast wall gave way and spilled onto Jefferson Street. This in turn caused the top section of its north wall to topple as well. But when the north wall separated, it fell directly onto the smaller building being searched by Chief

Leather lungs: firefighters brave smoke while battling a chuch fire in 1960 on the west side.

Kuhn, cutting off escape for Kuhn and a rookie firefighter who was with him. Initially the pair located a window; however, it was covered by burglar bars. Two side doors were also blocked, one by a semitrailer parked flush against the building, the other by a locked steel gate. With the entire building next door ready to fall on them, Kuhn made one last frantic call for help. "Get us out of here," he radioed his superiors outside. "We're caught."[6]

About 60 firefighters raced against time in a desperate attempt to free their imperiled colleagues. As one group worked feverishly to remove the bars from the window, another tried to force open the locked steel door. Several more scrambled to move the parked trailer truck. Not one of these efforts paid off, though, because at 7:03 A.M., the entire seven-story east wall of the burning building crumbled. When the dust cleared, the worst fears were realized. Dozens of injured and dazed firefighters lay in the street or beneath giant mounds of rubble. Others stumbled disoriented after being knocked unconscious. Soot-covered and bloody, the survivors surveyed the scene with stunned disbelief. Spread out before them was a tremendous spectacle of fire, smoke, debris, and death. Large timbers used to support the failed building had cracked in half like giant toothpicks while two fire trucks sat partially buried under pulverized bricks. Worse off than the men in the trucks were more than a dozen others caught in the collapse.

Digging in the January cold for buried comrades once again proved to be miserable work, especially when it was known that some were almost certainly dead. Yet for the next 15 hours, weary firefighters toiled in subzero temperatures to carefully dig a makeshift tunnel that led them to recover five bodies. When tunneling became too dangerous, heavy equipment was brought in to pick apart the ruins. Eventually the mutilated remains of four more firefighters were found, including Chiefs Rees and Kuhn, bringing the final death toll to nine.

WHENEVER A fire engine answers an alarm, those on board never know what to expect. Though they may have a general idea based on a caller's report and the latest pre-fire plan information, unseen hazards make each response an encounter into the unknown. On February 7, 1968, firefighters on Chicago's south side faced just such a situation. Before the evening was out, three of them would be dead, a fourth mortally hurt.

For most of the 100 people employed by the Mickelberry Food Products Company, the workday had ended at 4 P.M. that Wednesday. The plant at 801 W. 49th St. was located in a densely populated neighborhood just south of the Union Stockyards, and like many similar manufacturing buildings in the area, the large Mickelberry factory had an irregular layout. The entire complex measured 200 feet wide by 125 feet long and its office wing was two and three stories high. The adjacent sausage factory stood one story.

About 25 employees were still inside the factory when, at around 4:15 P.M., a gasoline tanker truck pulled into the alley behind it to deliver more than 600 gallons of gasoline to the company's underground fuel tanks. What happened next remains sketchy. Somehow, a valve on the right side of the truck struck a projection sticking out from the building's exterior, rupturing the gasoline tank and causing its contents to spill into the plant's basement furnace room. Fire soon broke out and the situation turned perilous. The frightened truck driver leaped from the cab and ran into the street calling for help. Two police officers noticed his frantic waving and yelling. "I hit something in the alley," the driver told them. "My truck's on fire."[7] After radioing for the fire department, the two officers jumped from their squad car and began clearing pedestrians from the crowded sidewalks.

Engine 50 and Hook-and-Ladder 18 quickly responded

A display case inside the Chicago Fire Academy contains more than 500 badges of firefighters killed in the line of duty since 1858.

for the 25 workers still caught inside the plant, forcing them to break through a door and flee to the roof. Because Truck 18's normal rig was in the shop that day, the company was running with a spare apparatus that did not have a working aerial ladder. Captain John Fischer and his crew instead threw up ground ladders to reach the trapped employees. Two firefighters climbed to the roof, while Fischer and four others began carrying the workers down one at a time.

Fourth Division Fire Marshal Robert Hart arrived a minute later, greeted by flames and charcoal black smoke shooting 50 feet into the air. Seeing the potential for disaster, Hart ordered a second alarm and asked police to evacuate occupants of nearby buildings. Also at risk was a large group of onlookers who had gathered along Halsted Street to watch the unfolding drama, including factory workers, school children, afternoon shoppers, and housewives. Unfortunately, there wasn't enough time for a widespread withdrawal, because at 4:27 P.M. (that's when clocks in the area stopped), the gasoline truck exploded and the Mickelberry plant blew apart, sending a huge fireball into the sky and hurling bodies, bricks, and glass in all directions. The concussion was so tremendous that it broke windows on buildings several blocks away. It also blew firefighters off ladders and those they were attempting to rescue off the roof. More than 100 bystanders had also been caught in the carnage. Bloodied and disfigured, their bodies lay everywhere, some on the street and sidewalk, others sprawled over cars toppled with debris. Some

from their nearby firehouse, and upon learning that a gasoline truck was burning in the alley, stretched two hoselines and began playing water on the soaring flames. More help was called when a series of small explosions began to erupt inside the building, producing flames and smoke that cut off escape had been killed instantly. The survivors crawled away. When the dust cleared, the scene along Halsted Street resembled a war zone. Concrete and glass littered the ground while vehicles that had been parked next to the building were tipped over or burning. It could've been London during the blitz or a town center in Northern Ireland following a terrorist blast. Instead it was Chicago on a busy and terrible afternoon.

The plant's office section as well as a large portion of the sausage factory had been demolished; the outer walls were blown out and most of the roof had collapsed. Fire Commissioner Robert J. Quinn assumed command and a 4-11 alarm was sounded to bring more help. Gas and electricity to the neighborhood was turned off and the city's disaster plan was put into effect. Firefighters used foam to extinguish most of the remaining fire and searchlights were brought in to aid rescuers. When the digging was completed there were nine dead and 77 injured. Most of those hurt were bystanders; the driver of the gasoline truck was taken to the hospital in serious condition. The dead included Mickelberry's president and four of the firefighters from Hook-and-Ladder 18 who had been working on ladders just before the explosion. One other victim was an 18-year-old high school student who, while walking home, had seen the fire and ran to help; he was steadying a ladder when the truck exploded.

IN THE years following the Mickelberry disaster, Chicago's firefighters continued to die at a steady pace, many alongside one another. On February 13, 1971, a "routine" fire in a light industrial building turned disastrous. Firefighters had been called to 6117 N. Elston Ave. after someone saw smoke rising from the rear of the structure. As firefighters began stretching a hose line in the building, they smelled a strong odor of natural gas. But before the source of the leak could be traced, the gas ignited, triggering a massive explosion that leveled most of the building. Firefighters standing outside were blown across the street, and a number of civilians were also injured. It took several hours for rescuers to recover the bodies of two firefighters who had died instantly. Less than two years later, on January 6, 1973, three more firefighters died when an overnight three-alarm fire swept the Forum Restaurant at 64 W. Madison St. in the Loop. Firefighters had the blaze extinguished and were overhauling the second-floor cafeteria when a hidden pocket of fire sparked a sudden flashover, causing the roof to fall in on them. On August 22, 1981, two more firefighters met equally horrible deaths. After becoming disoriented and lost in thick smoke during a fire in a downtown office building on Michigan Avenue, the pair made their way through a darkened hallway in search of an exit, only to unwittingly crawl into an open elevator shaft, where they plunged ten floors.

Tragedy was repeated on February 1, 1985, when a predawn fire broke out in a two-story building housing an electronics store near Diversey and Milwaukee Avenues on Chicago's northwest side. Firefighters were sent to the structure's snow-covered roof to cut a hole to release smoke and heat collecting inside when a sudden rumble was felt followed by a loud crack. Without warning the roof fell in, taking three members of Hook-and-Ladder 58 down into the flames. A fourth firefighter narrowly escaped death, but sustained burns over 20 percent of his body. It was later learned that the business owners had hired someone to start the fire in a scheme to collect $250,000 in insurance money. Another seemingly routine fire in an auto repair shop in April 1999 left two more firefighters dead. An unexpected flashover occurred as the pair was inside the south side building looking for the fire's source.

The lessons from these tragedies hopefully can be heeded to minimize their repeat. It doesn't take a genius to realize that firefighters should stay clear of teetering walls on fire-weakened structures, or that endangering firefighters to save old, worn-out buildings is a foolish gamble. Still, risk-taking is sometimes necessary, especially when lives are in jeopardy.

Before Chicago replaced its telegraph fire alarm with a modern computerized dispatch system, the signal 3-3-5 was tapped out each time a fire company returned to its quarters. Today, along with a bugler playing taps, that same 3-3-5 signal is rung ceremonially at funerals whenever a firefighter is laid to rest after making the "supreme sacrifice." Though the romance of the past may have given way to the technology of the present and future, the message of the bell remains the same:

The firefighter is home.

Notes

Chapter 1: From Dearborn to DeKoven

1. James S. McQuade, ed., *A Synoptical History of the Chicago Fire Department* (Chicago: Benevolent Association of the Paid Fire Department of Chicago, 1908), 7.

2. George Bushnell, "Chicago's Rowdy Firefighters," *Chicago History* (Autumn 1975): 232.

3. Ibid.

4. Ibid.

Chapter 2: Rise and Fall and Rise

1. David Lowe, ed., *The Great Chicago Fire* (New York: Dover, 1979), 64.

2. Richard Bales, "Did the Cow Do It?" *Illinois Historical Journal* (Spring 1997): 33.

Chapter 3: World's Columbian Exposition Fire

1. McQuade, 74.

Chapter 4: The Show Did Not Go On

1. *Chicago Tribune*, 31 December 1903.

Chapter 5: Disaster in the Stockyards

1. *Chicago Tribune*, 23 December 1910.

2. *Chicago Tribune*, 26 December 1910.

Chapter 6: The Hand of Death

1. Alex Burkholder, "April's Hand of Death," *Firehouse* (April 1983): 53.

Chapter 7: Hog Butcher to the World

1. John Costello, "Interview with Fire Marshall John Costello," *Chicago Firefighter* (March 1964): 34.

Chapter 8: LaSalle Hotel Fire

1. *Chicago Daily News*, 5 June 1946.

2. Ibid.

Chapter 9: Streetcar Named Disaster

1. Albert Peterson, "Interview with Assistant Fire Marshal Albert Peterson," *Chicago Firefighter* (March 1953): 23.

Chapter 10: No Vacancy

1. *Chicago Tribune*, 13 February 1955.

2. *Chicago Firefighter* (December 1955): 11.

Chapter 11: Legacy of the Angels

1. David Cowan and John Kuenster, *To Sleep With the Angels: The Story*

of a Fire (Chicago: Ivan R. Dee, 1996): 30.

2. Ibid., 32.

3. Ibid., 42.

4. Ibid., 179.

5. Ibid., 199.

6. Ibid., 211.

7. Ibid., 203.

Chapter 12: Fire and Ice

1. Miller, 101.

2. Chicago Fire Department audio tape of fire communications, 16 January 1967.

Chapter 13: A Burning Fury

1. *Chicago Tribune*, 5 April 1968.

2. Ibid.

3. Robert Freeman, "The West Side Riots: Countless Blazes, Hecklers, Looters Hamper Firemen," *Chicago Firefighter* (Fall 1968): 15-21.

4. *Chicago Tribune*, 5 April 1968.

5. *Chicago Tribune*, 6 April 1968.

6. *Chicago Tribune*, 10 April 1968.

7. Report by the U.S. National Advisory Commission on Civil Disorders (Kerner Report) (New York: Bantam Books, 1968).

Chapter 14: The City That Works

1. *Chicago Tribune*, 22 January 1909.

2. *Chicago Daily News*, 17 April 1953.

Chapter 15: Home Fires Burning

1. *Chicago Daily News*, 8 September 1953.

2. *Chicago Tribune*, 31 January 1976.

Chapter 16: In the Line of Duty

1. *Chicago Tribune*, 10 January 1918.

2. *Chicago Daily News*, 10 July 1943.

3. Ibid.

4. *Chicago Tribune*, 18 December 1953

5. Ibid.

6. Neal Callahan, "Chicago building collapse snuffs out lives of nine firefighters," *Fire Engineering* (April 1961): 286-304.

7. *Chicago Tribune*, 8 February 1968

Bibliography

Books

Bielski, Ursula. *Chicago Haunts: Ghostlore of the Windy City.* Chicago: Lake Claremont Press, 1998.

Bielski, Ursula, and Matt Hucke. *Graveyards of Chicago.* Chicago: Lake Claremont Press, 1999.

Bronstein, Don, and Tony Weitzel, eds. *Chicago: I Will.* Cleveland: The World Publishing Co., 1967.

Chafe, William H. *The Unfinished Journey: America Since World War II.* New York: Oxford University Press, 1991.

Cohen, Adam, and Elizabeth Taylor. *American Pharaoh: Mayor Richard J. Daley: His Battle for Chicago and the Nation.* New York: Little, Brown and Co., 2000.

Cowan, David, and John Kuenster. *To Sleep With the Angels: The Story of a Fire.* Chicago: Ivan R. Dee, 1996.

Cromie, Robert. *The Great Chicago Fire,* Illustrated Edition. Nashville: Rutledge Hill Press, 1994.

Cronon, William. *Nature's Metropolis: Chicago and the Great West.* New York: W.W. Norton, 1991.

Dedmon, Emmett. *Fabulous Chicago.* New York: Random House, 1953.

Dineen, Michael, ed. *Great Fires of America.* Waukesha, WI: Country Beautiful, 1973.

Ditzel, Paul. *Fire Engines, Firefighters.* New York: Crown Publishers, 1976.

Everett, Marshall. *The Great Chicago Theater Disaster.* Chicago: Publishers Union of America, 1904.

Goodspeed, E.J. *The Great Fires in Chicago and the West.* New York: H.S. Goodspeed & Co., 1871.

Griffin, Dick, and Rob Warden, eds. *Done in a Day: 100 Years of Great Writing From the Chicago Daily News.* Chicago: The Swallow Press, 1977.

Hayner, Don, and Tom McNamee. *Chicago Sun-Times Metro Chicago Almanac.* Chicago: Bonus Books, 1993.

Heise, Kenan, and Mark Frazel. *Hands on Chicago*. Chicago: Bonus Books, 1987.

Kotlowitz, Alex. *There are No Children Here*. New York: Doubleday, 1991.

Lanctot, Barbara. *A Walk Through Graceland Cemetery*. Chicago: Chicago Architecture Foundation, 1988.

Little, Ken, and John McNalis. *History of Chicago Firehouses of the 19th Century*. Chicago: Self-published, 1996.

——. *History of Chicago Firehouses, 1900-1925*. Chicago: Self-published, 2000.

Lindberg, Richard. *Quotable Chicago*. Chicago: Wild Onion Books, 1996.

—— *Return to the Scene of the Crime*. Nashville: Cumberland House, 1999.

Lowe, David, ed. *The Great Chicago Fire*. New York: Dover, 1979.

Miller, Donald. *City of the Century*. New York: Simon & Schuster, 1996.

McQuade, James S., ed. *A Synoptical History of the Chicago Fire Department*. Chicago: Benevolent Association of the Paid Fire Department of Chicago, 1908.

Pacyga, Dominic, and Ellen Skerrett. *Chicago, City of Neighborhoods*. Chicago: Loyola University Press, 1986.

Royko, Mike. *Boss: Richard J. Daley of Chicago*. New York: Dutton, 1971.

Sawyers, June. *Chicago Sketches*. Chicago: Wild Onion Books, 1995.

Smith, Dennis. *History of Firefighting in America*. New York: The Dial Press, 1978.

Starkey, David, and Richard Guzman, eds. *Smokestacks and Skyscrapers: An Anthology of Chicago Writing*. Chicago: Wild Onion Books, 1999.

Articles, Reports, and Other Materials

Babcock, Chester. "The Chicago School Fire." National Fire Protection Association (January 1959).

Bales, Richard. "Did the Cow Do It?" *Illinois Historical Journal* (Spring 1997).

Best, M. "The Wincrest Nursing Home Fire." National Fire Protection Association (September 1976).

Burkholder, Alex. "April's Hand of Death." *Firehouse* (April 1983).

Bushnell, George. "Chicago's Rowdy Firefighters." *Chicago History* (Autumn 1975).

Callahan, Neal. "Chicago building collapse snuffs out lives of nine firefighters." *Fire Engineering* (April 1961).

Chicago Board of Underwriters and the National Board of Fire Underwriters. *Report of Union Stockyard and Transit Company Conflagration*, 1934.

——. *Conflagration in Grain Elevators Operated by Rosenbaum Bros. Inc., and Norris Grain Company, Chicago, Illinois*, 1939.

Chicago Fire Department. *Fire Marshal's Annual Report*, 1903.
   Includes the findings of the Iroquois Theater fire investigation.

——. *Report of the Fire Marshal*, 1910.
   Includes information on the December 1910 stockyards fire.

Chicago Public Works Department. *Annual Report*, 1909.
   Includes excerpts from the fatal water crib fire.

Chicago Transit Authority. *Annual Report*, 1950.
   Includes excerpts of the investigation of the fatal streetcar accident.

——. ChicagoTransit Authority. *Transit News*, 1950.

Cook County (IL) Coroner. *Annual Report*, 1910.
   Includes a report on the fatal 1909 water crib fire.

——. *Findings of the Coroner's Jury in the Deaths of Victims of Our Lady of the Angels School Fire*, 1959.

Cook County (IL) Inspection Bureau. *Report of the LaSalle Hotel Fire*, 1946.

Ditzel, Paul. "Chicago '67: McCormick Place Inferno." *Firehouse* (October 1986).

——. "The Great Stockyards Fire." *Firehouse* (October 1989).

Doherty, Frank. "$40,000 Subscribed for Hero's Families." *Chicago Firefighter* (March 1954).

Eisner, Harvey. "On the Job: Chicago: Three Firefighters Killed." *Firehouse* (April 1985).

——. "On the Job: Chicago: Paxton Hotel Fire." *Firehouse* (July 1993).

Hashagen, Paul. "Chicago's World's Fair of 1893." *Firehouse* (July 1993).

Hoffman, Peter. *The Race Riots and Official Record of Inquests on the Victims of the Race Riots of July and August 1919.* Chicago: Cook County Coroner's Office Biennial Report 1918-1919, 1920.

Kennedy, John. *Investigation into the cause and origin of the Our Lady of the Angels school fire as prepared for the Catholic Archdiocese of Chicago.* Chicago: John Kennedy and Associates, Inc., 1959.

Transcript of 1962 interview with juvenile suspected of setting 1958 fire at Our Lady of the Angels school, conducted by John Reid. Provided by John Reid to John Kuenster and author.

Report of the Chicago Riot Study Committee to the Honorable Richard J. Daley. Chicago, 1968.

Report of the Investigation of the McCormick Place Fire, January 16, 1967. Chicago: Mayor's Committee to Investigate the McCormick Place Fire, 1967.

Report on the Investigation of the Wincrest Nursing Home Fire. Chicago: Special Panel Appointed by Chicago Mayor Richard J. Daley, 1976.

Report by the U.S. National Advisory Commission on Civil Disorders (Kerner Report). New York: Bantam Books, 1968.

Richards, Michael. "Tragedy on North Side." *Chicago Firefighter* (Autumn 1971).

Spehn, John. "Tragedy Strikes Chicago: Four Firefighters Die." *Chicago Firefighter* (Spring 1968).

Spencer, C.D. "Chicago's Second Great Fire." *The National Underwriter* (May 1934).

Photo Credits

Preface

1. Courtesy of the Chicago Public Library Special Collections Department.

Chapter 1: From Dearborn to DeKoven

1. From author's collection.

2. From author's collection.

3. Courtesy of the Chicago Public Library.

4. Courtesy of the Chicago Public Library.

5. Courtesy of the Chicago Public Library.

6. Courtesy of the Chicago Public Library.

7. From author's collection.

8. From author's collection.

Chapter 2: Rise and Fall and Rise

1. Courtesy of the Chicago Public Library.

2. Courtesy of the Chicago Public Library.

3. Courtesy of the Chicago Public Library.

4. Courtesy of the Chicago Public Library.

5. Courtesy of the Chicago Public Library.

6. Courtesy of the Chicago Public Library.

7. Courtesy of the Chicago Public Library.

8. Courtesy of the Chicago Public Library.

9. From author's collection.

10. From author's collection.

Chapter 3: World's Columbian Exposition Fire

1. Courtesy of the Chicago Public Library.

2. Courtesy of the Chicago Public Library.

3. Courtesy of the Chicago Public Library.

Chapter 4: The Show Did Not Go On

1. Courtesy of the *Chicago Tribune*.

2. From author's collection.

3. From author's collection.

4. From author's collection.

Chapter 5: Disaster in the Stockyards

1. Courtesy of the Chicago Public Library.

2. Courtesy of the Chicago Public Library.

3. Courtesy of the Chicago Public Library.

4. From author's collection.

5. From author's collection.

Chapter 6: The Hand of Death

1. Courtesy of the Chicago Public Library.

2. Courtesy of the Chicago Public Library.

3. Photo by David Berger.

Chapter 7: Hog Butcher to the World

1. Courtesy of the Chicago Public Library.

2. Photo by Edward Prendergast.

3. Photo by Edward Prendergast.

4. Photo by Edward Prendergast.

5. Photo by Edward Prendergast.

Chapter 8: LaSalle Hotel Fire

1. Associated Press.

2. Associated Press.

3. From author's collection.

Chapter 9: Streetcar Named Disaster

1. From author's collection.

2. Copyright by Steve Lasker.

3. From author's collection.

4. Copyright by Steve Lasker.

Chapter 10: No Vacancy

1. Courtesy of the Chicago Historical Society, ICHi-23204.

2. Courtesy of the Chicago Fire Department.

3. From author's collection.

4. From author's collection.

5. Courtesy of the Chicago Fire Department.

6. Photo by David Berger.

Chapter 11: Legacy of the Angels

1. From author's collection.

2. Courtesy of the Chicago Fire Department.

3. Courtesy of the Chicago Fire Department.

4. Courtesy of the Chicago Fire Department.

5. Courtesy of the Chicago Fire Department.

6. Courtesy of the Chicago Fire Department.

7. Photo by Bill Rowe.

Chapter 12: Fire and Ice

1. From author's collection.

2. Photo by Larry Steffens.

3. Photo by Larry Steffens.

4. Courtesy of the Chicago Fire Department.

5. Courtesy of the Chicago Fire Department.

Chapter 13: A Burning Fury

1. Courtesy of the Chicago Fire Department.

2. Photo by David Berger.

3. Photo by David Berger.

4. Courtesy of the Chicago Fire Department.

5. Photo by David Berger.

Chapter 14: The City That Works

1. Photo by David Berger.

2. Photo by Bud Bertog.

3. Photo by David Berger.

4. Photo by David Berger.

5. Photo by Scott Peterson.

6. Photo by David Berger.

Chapter 15: Home Fires Burning

1. Photo by David Berger.

2. Photo by Sandy Bertog.

3. Photo by Bud Bertog.

4. Photo by David Berger.

5. From author's collection.

Chapter 16: In the Line of Duty

1. Photo by Sandy Bertog.

2. Courtesy of the Chicago Fire Department.

3. Courtesy of the Chicago Fire Department.

4. Courtesy of the Chicago Fire Department.

5. Photo by Sandy Bertog.

6. Photo by Bud Bertog.

7. Courtesy of the Chicago Fire Department.

8. Photo by author.

Index

Numbers in italics refer to photographs.

About the Author

David Cowan was born in Chicago in 1963. He co-authored (with John Kuenster) the critically acclaimed book about the Our Lady of the Angels school fire, *To Sleep With the Angels: The Story of a Fire* (Ivan R. Dee, Inc.). A U.S. Air Force veteran and former award-winning newspaper reporter, he holds degrees in journalism and political science from Southern Illinois University. Now a firefighter and independent journalist, Mr. Cowan has written for major newspapers and magazines and appeared in numerous television documentaries about historic fires. He lives in Chicago with his wife, writer and historian Ursula Bielski, and their daughter, Eva.

Publisher's Credits

Cover design by Timothy Kocher. Interior design and layout by Sharon Woodhouse.
Editing by Bruce Clorfene. Proofreading by Sharon Woodhouse, Karen Formanski, Amy Formanski,
and Ken Woodhouse. Index by Karen Formanski. Production help from Carlo Buquiz.
The text of *Great Chicago Fires* was set in GoudyOld, with heads in Graupel.

Note

Although Lake Claremont Press and the author, editor, and others affiliated with *Great Chicago Fires*
have exhaustively researched all sources to ensure the accuracy and completeness of the information contained
within this book, we assume no responsibility for errors, inaccuracies, omissions, or inconsistencies herein.

Lake Claremont Press is . . .

The Chicago River: A Natural and Unnatural History
By Libby Hill

When French explorers Jolliet and Marquette used the Chicago portage on their return trip from the Mississippi River, the Chicago River was but a humble, even sluggish, stream in the right place at the right time. That's the story of the making of Chicago. This is the *other* story—the story of the making and perpetual re-making of a river by everything from geological forces to the interventions of an emerging and mighty city. Author Libby Hill brings together years of original research and the contributions of dozens of experts to tell the Chicago River's epic tale—and intimate biography—from its conception in prehistoric glaciers to the glorious rejuvenation it's undergoing today, and every exciting episode in between. **Winner of a 2000 Midwest Independent Publishers Association Award: Merit Award (2nd Place) in History!**
1-893121-02-X, August 2000, softcover, 302 pages, 78 historic and contemporary maps and photos, $16.95

Literary Chicago: A Book Lover's Tour of the Windy City
By Greg Holden, with foreword by Harry Mark Petrakis

Chicago has attracted and nurtured writers, editors, publishers, and book lovers for more than a century and continues to be one of the nation's liveliest literary cities. Join Holden as he journeys through the streets, people, ideas, events, and culture of Chicagoland's historic and contemporary literary world. Includes 11 detailed walking/driving tours.
1-893121-01-1, March 2001 , softcover, 332 pages, 83 photos, 11 maps, $15.95

"The Movies Are":
Carl Sandburg's Film Reviews and Essays, 1920-1928
Edited and with historical commentary by Arnie Bernstein, with introduction by Roger Ebert

During the 1920s, a time when movies were still considered light entertainment by most newspapers, the *Chicago Daily News* gave Sandburg a unique forum to express his views on the burgeoning film arts. *"The Movies Are"* compiles hundreds of Sandburg's writings on film, including reviews, interviews, and his earliest published essays of Abraham Lincoln—which he wrote for his film column. Take a new look at one of Hollywood's most exciting periods through the critical perspective of one of America's great writers. A passionate film advocate, Sandburg early on grasped and delighted in the many possibilities for the new motion picture medium, be they creative, humanitarian, or technological; intellectual, low-brow, or merely novel. In doing so, he began defining the scope and sophistication of future film criticism.
1-893121-05-4, October 2000, softcover, 397 pages, 72 historic photos and artifacts, $17.95

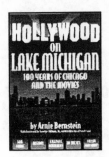

Hollywood on Lake Michigan: 100 Years of Chicago and the Movies

By Arnie Bernstein, with foreword by *Soul Food* writer/director George Tillman, Jr.

This engaging history and street guide finally gives Chicago and Chicagoans due credit for their prominent role in moviemaking history, from the silent era to the present. With trivia, special articles, historic and contemporary photos, film profiles, anecdotes, and exclusive interviews with dozens of personalities, including Studs Terkel, Roger Ebert, Gene Siskel, Dennis Franz, Harold Ramis, Joe Mantegna, Bill Kurtis, Irma Hall, and Tim Kazurinsky. **Winner of an American Regional History Publishing Award: 1st Place—Midwest!**

0-9642426-2-1, December 1998, softcover, 364 pages, 80 historic and contemporary photos, $15

Ghosts and Graveyards

Chicago Haunts: Ghostlore of the Windy City

By Ursula Bielski

From ruthless gangsters to restless mail order kings, from the Fort Dearborn Massacre to the St. Valentine's Day Massacre, the phantom remains of the passionate people and volatile events of Chicago history have made the Second City second to none in the annals of American ghostlore. Bielski captures over 160 years of this haunted history with her unique blend of lively storytelling, in-depth historical research, exclusive interviews, and insights from parapsychology. Called "a masterpiece of the genre," "a must-read," and "an absolutely first-rate-book" by reviewers, *Chicago Haunts* continues to earn the praise of critics and readers alike. **Our best-seller!**

0-9642426-7-2, October 1998, softcover, 277 pages, 29 photos, $15

More Chicago Haunts: Scenes from Myth and Memory

By Ursula Bielski

Chicago. A town with a past. A people haunted by its history in more ways than one. A "windy city" with tales to tell . . . Bielski is back with more history, more legends, and more hauntings, including the personal scary stories of *Chicago Haunts* readers. Read about the Ovaltine factory haunts, the Monster of 63rd Street's castle of terror, phantom blueberry muffins, Wrigley Field ghosts, Al Capone's yacht, and 45 other glimpses into the haunted myths and memories of Chicagoland.

1-893121-04-6, October 2000, softcover, 312 pages, 50 photos, $15

Haunted Michigan: Recent Encounters with Active Spirits
By Rev. Gerald S. Hunter

Within these pages you will not find ancient ghost stories or legendary accounts of spooky events of long ago. Instead, Rev. Hunter shares his investigations into modern ghost stories—active hauntings that continue to this day. *Haunted Michigan* uncovers a chilling array of local spirits in its tour of the two peninsulas. Wherever you may dwell, these tales of Michigan's ethereal residents are sure to make you think about the possibility, as Hunter suggests, that we are not always alone within the confines of our happy homes. So wait until the shadows of night have cast a pall over the serenity of your peaceful abode. Then snuggle into your favorite overstuffed chair, pour yourself a bracing bolt of 80-proof courage, and open your mind to the presence of the paranormal which surrounds us all.
1-893121-10-0, October 2000, softcover, 207 pages, 20 photos, $12.95

Graveyards of Chicago: The People, History, Art, and Lore of Cook County Cemeteries
By Matt Hucke and Ursula Bielski

Like the livelier neighborhoods that surround them, Chicago's cemeteries are often crowded, sometimes weary, ever-sophisticated, and full of secrets. They are home not only to thousands of individuals who fashioned the city's singular culture and character, but also to impressive displays of art and architecture, landscaping and limestone, egoism and ethnic pride, and the constant reminder that although physical life must end for us all, personal note—and notoriety—last forever.
0-9642426-4-8, November 1999, softcover, 228 pages, 168 photos, $15

Guidebooks by Locals

Ticket to Everywhere: The Best of Detours Travel Column
By Dave Hoekstra, with foreword by Studs Terkel

Chicago Sun-Times columnist Dave Hoekstra has compiled 66 of his best road trip explorations into the offbeat people, places, events, and history of the greater Midwest and Route 66 areas. Whether covering the hair museum in Independence, Missouri; Wisconsin's "Magical Mustard Tour"; the Ohio Tiki bar on the National Register of Historic Places; Detroit's polka-dot house; or Bloomington, Illinois—home to beer nuts, Hoekstra's writings will delight readers and instruct tourists.
1-893121-11-9, November 2000, softcover, 227 pages, 70 photos, 9 maps, $15.95

A Native's Guide to Chicago, 3rd Edition
By Sharon Woodhouse, with expanded South Side coverage by Mary McNulty
Venture into the nooks and crannies of everyday Chicago with this unique, comprehensive budget guide. Over 400 pages of free, inexpensive, and unusual things to do in the Windy City make this the perfect resource for tourists, business travelers, visiting suburbanites, and resident Chicagoans. Called the "best guidebook for locals" in *New City*'s 1999 "Best of Chicago" issue!
0-9642426-0-5, January 1999, softcover, 438 pages, photos, maps, $12.95

Whether you're a life-long resident, new in town, or just passing through, let the Native's Guide series for Chicago's suburban regions be your personal tour guides of the best our suburbs have to offer.

A Native's Guide to Chicago's Northern Suburbs
By Jason Fargo
0-9642426-8-0, June 1999, softcover, 207 pages, photos, maps, $12.95

A Native's Guide to Chicago's Northwest Suburbs
By Martin A. Bartels
1-893121-00-3, August 1999, softcover, 315 pages, photos, maps, $12.95

A Native's Guide to Chicago's Western Suburbs
By Laura Mazzuca Toops and John W. Toops, Jr.
0-9642426-6-4, August 1999, softcover, 210 pages, photos, maps, $12.95

A Native's Guide to Chicago's South Suburbs
by Christina Bultinck and Christy Johnston-Czarnecki
0-9642426-1-3, June 1999, softcover, 242 pages, photos, maps, $12.95

A Native's Guide to Northwest Indiana
By Mark Skertic
1-893121-08-9, Spring 2002

Full of the fascinating sights, places, stories, and facts that sometimes even locals don't know about, the Native's Guide series equips you with everything you need to enjoy and navigate Chicago and its suburbs like a true insider.

Order Form

Title		Price	
Great Chicago Fires	_____	@ $19.95 =	_____
The Chicago River	_____	@ $16.95 =	_____
Literary Chicago	_____	@ $15.95 =	_____
"The Movies Are"	_____	@ $17.95 =	_____
Hollywood on Lake Michigan	_____	@ $15.00 =	_____
Chicago Haunts	_____	@ $15.00 =	_____
More Chicago Haunts	_____	@ $15.00 =	_____
Haunted Michigan	_____	@ $12.95 =	_____
Graveyards of Chicago	_____	@ $15.00 =	_____
Ticket to Everywhere	_____	@ $15.95 =	_____
A Native's Guide to Chicago	_____	@ $12.95 =	_____
. . . Northern Suburbs	_____	@ $12.95 =	_____
. . . Northwest Suburbs	_____	@ $12.95 =	_____
. . . Western Suburbs	_____	@ $12.95 =	_____
. . . South Suburbs	_____	@ $12.95 =	_____

Subtotal: _____

Less Discount: _____

New Subtotal: _____

8.75% Sales Tax for Illinois Residents: _____

Shipping: _____

TOTAL: _____

Discounts when you order several titles!
2 books—10% off total, 3-4 books—20% off,
5-9 books—25% off, 10+ books—40% off

—Low shipping fees—
$2.50 for the first book and $.50 for each additional book,
with a maximum charge of $6.

Order by mail, phone, fax, or e-mail.
All of our books have a no-hassle,
100% money back guarantee.

*Lake Claremont Press books can be
found at Chicagoland bookstores and
online at Amazon.com, bn.com, and others.*

Name_____

Address_____

City_____**State**_____**Zip**_____

E-mail Address _____

*Please enclose check, money order,
or credit card information.*

Visa/Mastercard #_____**Exp.** _____

Signature_____

4650 N. Rockwell St.
Chicago, IL 60625
773/583-7800
773/583-7877 (fax)
lcp@lakeclaremont.com
www.lakeclaremont.com

LAKE CLAREMONT PRESS

Also from Lake Claremont Press

Literary Chicago:
A Book Lover's Tour of the Windy City
by Greg Holden

"The Movies Are": Carl Sandburg's
Film Reviews and Essays, 1920-1928
ed. by Arnie Bernstein,
introduction by Roger Ebert

Hollywood on Lake Michigan:
100 Years of Chicago and the Movies
by Arnie Bernstein

The Chicago River:
A Natural and Unnatural History
by Libby Hill

Ticket to Everywhere:
The Best of Detours *Travel Column*
by Dave Hoekstra

Graveyards of Chicago: The People, History,
Art, and Lore of Cook County Cemeteries
by Matt Hucke and Ursula Bielski

Chicago Haunts:
Ghostlore of the Windy City
by Ursula Bielski

More Chicago Haunts:
Scenes from Myth and Memory
by Ursula Bielski

Haunted Michigan:
Recent Encounters with Active Spirits
by Rev. Gerald S. Hunter

A Native's Guide to Chicago
by Sharon Woodhouse, with South Side
coverage by Mary McNulty

A Native's Guide to
Chicago's Northern Suburbs
by Jason Fargo

A Native's Guide to
Chicago's Northwest Suburbs
by Martin A. Bartels

A Native's Guide to
Chicago's Western Suburbs
by Laura Mazzuca Toops and
John W. Toops, Jr.

A Native's Guide to
Chicago's South Suburbs
by Christina Bultinck and
Christy Johnston-Czarnecki

Coming Soon

A Cook's Guide to Chicago
by Marilyn Pocius

West Side Stories:
Struggles for Community in Chicago's
Maxwell Street Neighborhood
by Carolyn Eastwood

Treading on Ancient Ground:
Native American Mounds Around Chicago
by Christina Bultinck and Nicole Bultinck

Chicago Haunts (Spanish Edition)
by Ursula Bielski

Chicago Haunts (Audiobook)
by Ursula Bielski

A Native's Guide to Northwest Indiana
by Mark Skertic

The Civil War in Chicago
by Arnie Bernstein

Chicago's Midway Airport:
The First Seventy-Five Years
by Christopher Lynch